MW01125480

bright. But none of it was aligned. I was tired and unsure. Who knew all I needed was Jennifer — a gifted, glittering guru — and Jeff— the kindest, most empathetic, and thoughtful midwestern dad — to open my heart and mind to the path I'm on today. Now, I'm more passionate than ever. I'm purpose-driven. I know what's possible, and I'm going to make it happen. My light is bigger and brighter than it's ever been. They helped me find alignment, and I'm leaning in. It's Go Time. With this book, anyone can exponentially grow their impact on the world, and the world desperately needs it.

**Derek Allen, Executive Vice President &
Chief Operating Officer, Starr Commonwealth**

For years, I have told friends near and far who were at a crossroads and looking for direction that they should attend a Lantern Retreat with Jennifer and Jeff. The problem was, when you're at a crossroads, the timing, money, or motivation can prove elusive. Now, Jennifer and Jeff have given us **Leading with Light** *to help reorient ourselves right when we need it, to help us get through, and to refer to throughout our journey.*

**Evelyn Furse, Summit County Clerk,
former U.S. Magistrate Judge**

I've participated in Plenty's signature Lantern program individually and also brought my company leadership team to Jeff and Jennifer, who led us through Meridian, their outstanding strategy retreat. In both cases, we were required to bring our full selves to the process, including our emotions, which is unique in business. In their new book, **Leading with Light***, Jeff and Jennifer share their personal journeys and guide readers into deep personal reflection. Through exercises and practices, the authors encourage you to courageously express your best self and let your presence shine—not just at work—but in all areas of your life. I highly recommend this book.*

Liam Killeen, CEO, Wells Enterprises, Inc.

Leading with Light *is the perfect book for a world of people yearning for more. Through profound and personal insights, exercises, and practices, Jennifer and Jeff take a fresh approach to leadership by bringing us back to the person who matters most: ourselves. In a time when we're all told to do more and be more, the invitation to become more aware, aligned, and intentional to the light within is a breath of fresh air. I highly recommend this book.*

**Tom Bufalino, General Manager,
James B. Beam Distilling Company**

Leading with Light *is the go-to guide for conscious leaders looking to make a positive difference in their lives and in the lives of those they lead. Jennifer and Jeff's natural light and positivity jump out of every page. Reading this book is like sipping a warm cup of soup on a cold winter day.*

Elaine Martyn, Senior Vice President, Fidelity Charitable

In a time of great uncertainty, **Leading with Light** *comes along as a wonderful reminder that we each have what we need to navigate what's before us. Jennifer and Jeff inspire us to bring our whole selves to work and life, trusting we have everything we need to lead the way. I highly recommend this rich and inspiring book.*

Ellie Starr, CEO/Founder, Starrs Aligned

LEADING
WITH
LIGHT

Choosing Conscious Leadership
When You're Ready for More

Jennifer Mulholland and Jeff Shuck

Principals of Plenty Consulting, Inc.

modern wisdom
PRESS

Modern Wisdom Press

Crestone, Colorado, USA

www.modernwisdompress.com

ISBN: 978-1-951692-36-0 (paperback), 978-1-951692-37-7 (epub)

DISCLAIMER

To our families, friends, clients,
and all conscious leaders everywhere.

Thank you!

J & J

THE FOUR LIGHTS OF CONSCIOUS LEADERSHIP

I — YOU ARE LIGHT

II — YOUR LIGHT IS ALWAYS ON

III — YOU ONLY HAVE TO SEE WHAT'S RIGHT IN FRONT OF YOU

IV — THERE'S A LARGER LIGHT GUIDING YOU

Contents

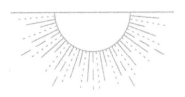

Foreword

Today, give yourself the gift of exhale.

Feel ease.

Because, kind stranger, you are worthy of wholeness.

And you're holding the path to reaching that peace in your hands.

What's nestled within the pages before you is an invitation to a journey toward becoming a whole leader—one who embraces the humanity within others and yourself.

For over two decades, the extraordinary authors have guided individuals and organizations in cultivating conscious leadership. Through their work at Plenty Consulting, their retreats at HeartSpace, and now, in this heart-wired book you're holding, they've illuminated a path toward replenishing ourselves and society.

Jennifer and Jeff first met in the tech sector in the '90s, recognizing in each other a shared passion for service and personal growth. Years later, they reconnected and co-founded Plenty to expand their vision of a world with "plenty for everyone." Through their wisdom and hands-on practice, they've helped thousands of leaders tap into their fullest potential. We're two of them.

We first saw them teach three years ago and started listening to their podcast, following their socials, and subscribed to their content. Finally, we had enough people in our two worlds telling us we needed to meet and giving us stories about each other that it felt like a reunion among friends when we finally met. And that was the day they came to record an episode on our podcast.

In our work at We Are For Good, we interview, story tell, and connect some of the most inspired changemakers of our generation. We meet a motley crew of characters—empaths, entrepreneurs, activists, quiet Do-Gooders, the vulnerable, and the most generative humans who sit in their frailty and power to do good. And when we met Jeff and Jen, the world tilted on its axis a bit. You know that feeling of meeting someone extra special and how it just shifts something within you? That's the feeling of wholeness and light these two humans add to your life.

At the core of their approach is a shift from scarcity to abundance. By believing in cooperation over competition and gratitude for what we have, they show how to solve problems and thrive sustainably. We were most struck by the concepts unpacked here—like those of awareness, alignment, and intention—each providing frameworks to understand ourselves and lead consciously.

With powerful tools such as cultivating presence through stillness and noticing our emotions, *Leading with Light* guides us to rediscover our light—that essence beyond mind and body, calling us to positive change. This book outlines and manifests a world of plenty for all by showing us how to look within and without for goodness.

As you read their raw stories of challenge and growth, you'll see how Jennifer and Jeff model vulnerability and wisdom. Through their work curating conversations with innovators in business and nonprofits, they nurture a community uplifting each other. By sharing their insights more broadly through these pages, they empower us all to lead with compassion through uncertain times. And even better, they invite us to reflect on how to replenish ourselves while serving others.

May their words illuminate a path toward conscious leadership, abundance, and light for all. Because light only emits more, you know, plenty. That's what Jennifer and Jeff impart to you in the following pages: light, love, more, plenty, wholeness, ease, and fulfillment in oneself, which is where we all should start—inside. And guess what—you're worthy of it. So, consider this your guidebook for the journey. You're in the gentlest and caring of hands.

Jennifer once shared with us the concept that **intention is expansion**. Welcome to the journey of expanding your leadership, your growth, and your heart in tandem.

How do we know? We're living proof that the teachings you'll discover inside *Leading with Light* are a powerful conductor with the ability to cast ripples. We're excited to see how your ripple adds to the abundance here for the taking, compounding for all of us.

Happy sojourn, fellow traveler. We're all rooting for you.

Jon + Becky
Co-founders, We Are For Good®

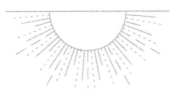

Introduction

A Long Time Coming

This book has been in our hearts and minds for decades. It's shown up on our dream boards, vision statements, and goal-setting exercises for years and years. It's something we've both talked about, wished for, and wanted since we were young.

As years passed, we got tired of hearing ourselves talk about writing our first book. As happens in life, one of our greatest dreams became a tease, then an annoyance, and then a weight. The cues showed up in subtle ways, as they often do. Both avid readers and collectors of books, we found ourselves not wanting to purchase them anymore. Walking into bookstores or hearing the book recommendations of others began to bring out a sense of subtle envy, frustration, and a bit of resentment.

We felt a stirring, individually and collectively. How were these other authors able to overcome such emotions? We began to see that we avoided the obstacle of writing a book by putting other projects first. Client commitments, upcoming retreats, team needs, family needs, social engagements, and everything else under the sun somehow always became more important than starting the book.

There was no "one point" that we suddenly became ready. Like the ideas we talk about in the following pages, the book emerged slowly. We worked with several consultants until we found the right one. We tried a few different subjects until we found the one that felt right. We drafted dozens of outlines on the way to map the book out. But in taking these steps, we created our own momentum. After over a decade of co-creating our company, co-leading our services and retreats, and committing to practice what we teach others, we were finally ready.

We have grown to trust the divine timing. This creation has been no different. The signs all around us were showing us it was time.

The idea of signs and symbols may sound silly, but they show up in our lives every day. Being aware of those signs and intentionally choosing how to respond is one of the practices of being a conscious leader. Paying attention and noticing the cues, whispers, synchronicities, and nudges from the Universe, God, Spirit, Source, Nature—whatever you may name it to be—is a mysterious, powerful, and fun way to navigate the path. Sometimes, the signs and nudges are blatantly obvious. Other times, the signs may be so subtle that we almost don't notice them.

Being, Not Doing

That kind of awareness is one of the core ideas of this book. Another core idea is connection. Fostering connection—connection to our own light, connection to something greater, and connection to others—is at the heart of why we are writing this book.

You see, most leadership books (and approaches and classes and schools) are built on the idea that there is a certain set of things you need to "do" to become a better leader. The thinking is that there is a set of guidelines that great leaders follow. We've studied much of that work, and we like a lot of it.

But the thing is, no one set of guidelines can tell you what is important to you. In fact, the whole idea that leadership is just about what you *do* feels outdated to us. This book is about helping you *be* more of *you*.

Maybe you have a growing sense that what used to be important to you doesn't feel like enough anymore. Maybe you want to connect to your team in a way that feels more authentic to who you are. Maybe you feel you are meant for something more. Maybe you feel like life has more to offer you. Maybe you realize you have more to offer life.

We have written this book to help you feel peace, confidence, and clarity about who you are, what works for you, and what you are here to do. We do that by sharing what has guided our way on the path of conscious leadership. As we do, we are acutely aware that what we share with you is equally meant for ourselves. That, by the way, is one of the simplest performance hacks in life—simply listen to the advice you give others, and take that wisdom for yourself. When you do, you'll become the leader you've been looking for.

We've come to the principles we extend to our clients by living and learning them. They emerged to us through a combined sixty years of helping people reach their potential.

Together, over the past ten years, we've had the privilege of combining our experience and dreams to co-lead Plenty. Simply put, at Plenty, we help conscious leaders and businesses grow. We do it by helping them develop strategies that are more purpose-driven, unlock profitable growth, create more fulfilling work, and build healthy, high-performing cultures.

Living Lantern

As we write this, we are concluding our eighth year and eighteenth session of Lantern, our retreat for conscious leaders. We facilitate and host Lantern at HeartSpace, our private retreat center in beautiful Park City, Utah (www.plentyconsulting. com/lantern). Leaders like you come from all over the world to spend four days to be reinspired about how to be. It's an inside-out approach to leadership development that includes a 360-degree leadership assessment, a facilitated curriculum, a beautiful unconference space, and our Lantern Leadership Model, designed to help participants articulate their unique blueprint. By "unique blueprint" we mean the fundamental questions that end up defining our lives: What do I really care about? What is my purpose? What is the highest possibility for my life?

The Lantern Leadership Retreat has been our playground for what you're about to read—and we have deep gratitude for the hundreds of remarkable, thoughtful, successful, and introspective leaders who have attended it. We've found that the practices of being a conscious leader—what we call the Four Principles of Conscious Leadership—serve as an easy guide for people who want to navigate life with more awareness, alignment, and intentionality. The principles become a kind of leadership touchstone—when we use them, our lives become lighter, freer, and more fulfilling than we could have ever imagined them to be. This is the blessing of our path, and we want to share that blessing with you.

We invite you to practice along with us as you read. The most important conversation is the one you have with yourself at every moment. After many of the chapters, we've added exercises to help you expand on not only the ideas in the book, but on your own conversation.

May the principles and pages that follow literally and figuratively light you up.

You are ready. You are all that is needed to light the way.

You are the light you seek.

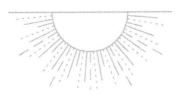

CHAPTER 1

A Crisis of Consciousness

Katie was late.

We were sitting in HeartSpace, our retreat center in Park City, ready to start a coaching session with her. We had hot coffee, open space, and calm music—everything we needed to begin. Except for Katie.

This wasn't like her. We had known Katie for a long time. An accomplished professional with a private practice, she was superb at balancing the many demands on her time—patients, team members, family, friends, volunteer commitments. From an outsider's perspective, she seemed to be at the top of her game.

So, when she had reached out a couple of months earlier about engaging in coaching with us, we were a bit surprised. Katie represented the kind of conscious leader we love to work with, but we couldn't see any of the signs of stress, dissatisfaction, or yearning we commonly find in leaders looking to grow. We said, "Of course—what would you like to work on?"

"I'm not sure," she said. "I've achieved everything I've ever set out to. But . . . ." She trailed off for a second. "I don't know. Something's missing."

Over the previous few months, we had really enjoyed getting to know Katie and had come to appreciate her thoughtfulness and depth. But after several coaching sessions, we still couldn't quite pinpoint why she had asked us to work with her. Now, sitting on the cozy couches of HeartSpace, we wondered as we waited about what might be holding her up—literally and figuratively.

A few minutes later, she arrived. Before we saw her face, we could sense the rush of someone flustered. The front door opened quickly and shut with a slam. She walked into our main room with her coat still on, complete with a thin scarf to provide some warmth in the Park City spring. She absently dropped her scarf onto the floor and collapsed into the sofa.

Katie looked tired. Frazzled. She seemed almost dim, in some way, like someone had turned down her brightness a few notches.

Jennifer asked, "Do you need a few moments to slow down and get here?"

Katie gave a nervous laugh. "Jeez, what a morning. Holy smokes. You know, when you're raising your kids, you tell yourself that things will get easier—and less expensive—when they grow up. Ha! I can't seem to catch up."

She paused. We could see tears welling up in her eyes.

"I mean, with the business, the kids, my marriage . . . it's so much. Everything is moving at warp speed. I feel like I'm running to stand still."

The World Is Speeding Up

We hear comments like Katie's all the time. Do you feel it? Does it seem like the world is speeding up?

Maybe you notice the pace in the news cycle, which seems to bring us a new world-shaking event every few weeks. "Once-in-a-lifetime" environmental incidents occur almost every month now. Domestic and global political tensions dominate the headlines. The financial and economic foundations of our world can seem to be on shakier ground every day.

Or do you notice the speed in your ever-present mobile device, constantly pushing notifications at you, telling you to be more, share more, do more, buy more?

Do you see it in your calendar, packed with things to do from sun-up to sun-down each and every day?

Do you see it in your bank account? A feeling like you're running to stand still, that no matter how much you learn and earn, your expenses always seem to just outpace your savings?

Or do you notice the pace in the conversations you have with your friends and family? Does it seem like despite the fact that we have more ways to connect with one another than ever before, our feelings of loneliness, isolation, and depression are at record highs?

For many, the pace of life is speeding up. And with that speed may come a sense of unease. It feels like the technological progress that has created so much prosperity is also personally running us into the ground.

There's Something More

And yet, doesn't it sometimes seem like there's more possibility than ever before, too? Perhaps hidden just beneath the surface, like a springtime tulip trying to push its way out of the frost on the ground?

Can you hear the whispers of a better world calling?

It could be in the growing proportion of electric vehicles you see in your neighborhood, or in the growing number of articles you read about the low-cost renewable energies now available.

Maybe it is in conversations with your kids, as you realize they have a much broader sense of tolerance and acceptance than you did when you were young.

Maybe it comes when you notice the growing number of mainstream podcasts that you listen to that mention the power of mindfulness, whole-body wellbeing, and mental health.

Maybe it is in catching a news story from the corner of your eye about the progress toward landing a human crew on Mars in our lifetime.

A new paradigm is emerging. Everywhere around us, the old systems of our world—many based on efficiency and hierarchy—are gasping for breath. That can feel disruptive and painful.

But new systems are taking their place—systems based on cooperation, respect, constructive creativity, and wellbeing. These systems are going to help us create a different kind of world, a world where the best aspects of technology integrate with the power of the natural world to uplift us all.

That feels like possibility.

People are realizing, "There's more out there."

And you're one of those people, aren't you?

Wanting More

This paradigm shift is personal, too. Many of us, like Katie, climbed a ladder. The shared experience of the global pandemic accelerated a quiet trend we've noticed for years: more and more people are taking stock of their work and their lives. And more and more people are deciding something is missing.

In our work with executives and leadership teams, we hear this story repeated frequently. We climb the ladder to success, and many of us—partly thanks to hard work, partly thanks to privilege, and partly thanks to good luck—are pleasantly surprised to realize we've ended up toward the top.

Most of the people we work with are tremendously accomplished. They are proud of their work. But once they get where they thought they wanted to go, they have a feeling that there's still something more waiting. We hear leaders say, "I think life has more to offer me."

And of course, the corollary to that belief is "I think I have more to offer life."

When Success Isn't Enough

Can you remember the last time you felt really, truly fulfilled?

Close your eyes and imagine it. Perhaps you finished a massive product launch with a team you had handpicked. Or finally broke ninety after trying to learn to play golf all summer. Maybe it was watching your child graduate from high school, seeing them grow into a real human, and knowing you played a part in that. Maybe it was finally earning your high school diploma after years of thinking you'd never go back to school. Maybe it was being on vacation, unplugged from your daily routine and feeling the freedom of limitless choice. Or perhaps it was looking at your life partner and realizing you found someone who you can be yourself around.

Whatever it was, can you recall the feeling?

Chances are that your feeling of fulfillment didn't come from doing something someone else *told* you to do—a.k.a. recognition. Now, don't get us wrong—giving and receiving praise is incredibly important, particularly for leaders. But true *fulfillment* comes from inside of you. Fulfillment comes from doing something you *chose* to do. And often, fulfillment comes from the *process* as much as the product.

When we reflect on the moments when we've really felt fulfilled, we recall our entire journey. Finding that life partner also means struggling with people who don't understand you. Raising a healthy adult means putting up with some unbearable teenage moments. Shooting ninety means playing some truly uninspired rounds of golf! Earning your high school diploma as an adult means overcoming challenges of workload, time management, and sometimes self-doubt.

Fulfillment comes from following what you love, through thick and thin, and learning something about yourself in the process.

Most of us didn't get to pick our grade school or the subjects we studied. Most of us didn't really pick whether we wanted to work— we knew that we had to put food on the table. *And so, we did our best with what we had to do, which is very, very different from doing our best at what we love to do.*

That paradigm shifts im'mediately when you realize "I could choose."

More and more people are waking up to the choices they have in their own lives. You don't simply *have* to take that next promotion. You don't have to stay at your current company at all, do you? Or even stay in your current field, right? You don't have to settle for your current relationship. Or choose to be overtired. Or underfulfilled.

The belief that you have a choice is a powerful thing. Our experience working with leaders has taught us that this idea of choice is as daunting as it is liberating. It is often harder to slow down when you reach a fork in the road than it is to keep grinding down your path when you don't have a choice.

But as scary as it might be, when you start to hear a voice inside your heart asking, "Is there more for me to become?" it's time to slow down and listen. Because the thing is, the question wouldn't even occur to you if there wasn't.

We Live One Life

There's a phrase we use every day at Plenty: *We live one life.* It's probably always been true, but in our ever-faster, ever-connected world, we don't have a "personal life" and a "professional life." Those are artificial constructs that were used to get us to think differently during the work week so we'd be more productive when on the job: Set your emotions aside until Friday night. Put off your passions until the weekend.

But these two lives aren't separate. You live one life.

If you've ever thought about an argument with your spouse while at work, or dragged a bad work conversation home with you and unwittingly taken it out on your kids, you've experienced the full-heart, full-self humanity we're talking about.

You live one life.

The more you try to segment it, divide it, and parcel it out, the more you end up feeling unfulfilled, disconnected, and lost.

You don't live a personal or professional life—you live one life. That's why, no matter how good you are at climbing the ladder, if it isn't a ladder you genuinely *want* to climb, you won't feel fulfilled when you get to the top.

And you'll be exhausted if you try. The more you try to keep your lives separate—showing up one way personally and a different way professionally—the more you will be sucked dry of your vital energy.

If you're the common denominator in both your personal life and professional lives, why not be your whole, authentic self in both places? And if you can't, for any reason, isn't that a cue to find the place where you can?

For each of us, the question isn't "How do I get to the top?" The question is "What do I love enough to keep me fulfilled in the climbing, no matter where I end up?"

And ironically, the wonderful truth is the more we focus on *what we love*, instead of *what we'll get*, the more we will create abundance that we can experience along the way. The *climb* can become the top, each and every day.

Not convinced? You don't have to be. But the fact that you've read this far shows us you have a sense that there's more for you to become.

The Invitation

Many stories of personal growth and transformation, ours included, start with what we call "The Mack Truck Moment"— something that comes from out of the blue and smacks you down so hard that you have no choice but to pay attention. Maybe you've already had such a moment: a cancer diagnosis, an injury that forced you to rest, a difficult divorce, or getting fired from a job that you later realized you never really liked. Experiences like these are catalysts for self-awareness. They are crucibles that can help us realize, "Maybe I want to live my life with more intention."

But we believe you don't need to wait for the harsh alarm. Life is inviting you, every moment, to wake up. The simple fact that you read the back flap of this book and thought, "Yes, I feel there might be more for me," is confirmation that there *is* something more available to you.

When you start to wonder if you're ready for more, you are.

It starts with a powerful question: What am I here to express?

This question will lead us into the fundamentals of conscious leadership we'll explore next:

- The call to be aware.

- The choice to be aligned.

- The opportunity to be intentional.

PRACTICE POINTS

Getting Started

Threaded between chapters, we offer practices designed to deepen your engagement with the ideas in the text. We invite you to try them out as you encounter them after each chapter. It is our hope that these questions and exercises give you the opportunity to feel increasingly in touch with your light as a leader. You may wish to have a notebook and pen around for some of these activities.

Here's one to start.

The Roles You Play

Take a moment to reflect on the many roles you currently play in work and life. We don't mean the titles you hold—we mean the roles within those titles.

For example, you may hold the title of "vice president of marketing." That title may come with many roles: visionary, inspirer, manager, PowerPoint maker, protector, convincer, and advocate. As another example, you may hold the title of "mother," which also brings with it many roles: caregiver, picker-upper, coach, coordinator, planner, yes-or-no-er, and approver.

As a way to examine the one life you get to live, write down all the roles you can think of that you've taken on in recent years.

- What roles do you see?

- How many roles are you playing?

- Are your work roles different from your personal roles? How?

- What roles feel fulfilling to you?

Bringing your own awareness to the many hats you wear in life is the first step toward aligning around what is really working for you—a process we'll consider in future chapters.

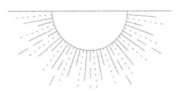

CHAPTER 2

Our Path to
Conscious Leadership

When we at Plenty talk about living a life of purpose, we can mistakenly give the impression that we knew what we were doing from the outset, that our lives moved down a single, straight, predetermined path, like an arrow flying toward its target. That couldn't be further from the truth.

Our own careers, and really our entire lives, have grown the way a tree grows: there was a period of expansion, of reaching up into the sky, followed by hardening as new tools and experiences were solidified and set in place. There were also periods of rest, and sometimes contraction, as we made mistakes and learned from them—and sometimes didn't learn from them, so we made them again.

As we've worked with leaders like you, we've realized that we aren't unique. When you look back on your life, can you see your own growth rings? Each time you experience a victory or a challenge, your tree of life changes—sometimes shedding things, other times contracting. Sometimes the growth contorts around obstacles, sometimes it absorbs them, and often it is permanently changed by them.

In the next couple of pages, we offer the stories of a couple of pivotal growth moments in our own lives. Our goal isn't to talk about ourselves, but rather to show you that we all grow in fits and starts. Our hope is that you'll recognize yourself in the experiences we share—our successes and our mistakes.

Spirituality in the Closet

JEN'S STORY:

I grew up in a family of healers and female entrepreneurs in the health and wellness industries. As a young girl, I learned Reiki, Theta Healing, energy work, and other healing disciplines from my mother, grandmother, and several other master teachers. From the earliest age, I knew that healing, leadership, and entrepreneurship were deeply woven into my way of being.

Inheriting my family's passion for athletics, I also loved expressing myself through sports. I followed that path through high school as an All-American and into college, playing lacrosse and field hockey for the University of Delaware. I was driven to excel and always found myself the captain of the team.

Over time, I began to feel called to something more. At the time, there were no professional lacrosse opportunities for women after college, and without that option, I wasn't sure what was next for me. One day, I took out a map of the United States and discovered Salt Lake City—close to skiing, the mountains, and nature, three of my favorite loves. Taking a leap of faith (that would turn out to be the first of many), I decided to make the move out west.

I loved Utah and the changes it brought me. And yet, something was still missing. Shortly after arriving there, I found myself at a bar one night, standing there with tears running down my face. A lacrosse game was playing on the television screen. It hit me like a ton of bricks—a deep sense of loss and longing. I missed the sport I had left behind in Delaware. My heart ached for it.

Lacrosse as a sport didn't exist in any organized way in the state for women, so I mustered my entrepreneurial drive to found a nonprofit to bring women's lacrosse to Utah. Through the organization, Women's Wasatch Lacrosse, I taught more than the sport—I taught leadership, teamwork, and initiative to women ranging from six to sixty, on and off the field.

I also taught the girls and women I coached how to interpret dreams, develop their intuition, and trust their instincts. It felt wonderful to combine the spiritual practices I valued so much with work I loved.

Women's Wasatch Lacrosse opened new connections and opportunities for me. As my career progressed, my love of combining leadership and consciousness, spirituality and business, coaching and strategy, deepened rather than diminished. My career led me to a technology start-up company, Campus Pipeline, where I first met Jeff. Campus Pipeline was formed in the first heyday of the tech boom— its mission was to create a digital campus for higher

*education worldwide (before there was such thing as the
.edu). It was fast, challenging, and fulfilling. I loved it!*

*Jeff and I spent an incredible two years developing a trust-
ing, collaborative team and a partnership we'd later build
on. We recruited a passionate team of idealistic people and
learned how to harness passion for growth. After roughly
two years, Jeff moved on (more on that below), but I stayed
and climbed higher, as the company grew through acqui-
sitions and mergers to become a Fortune 500 company.
I was eventually promoted to general manager of enterprise
consulting and innovation officer for the company. I was
respected, successful, and seemingly at the top of my career.*

Except . . .

*Over time, I felt that I wasn't expressing my whole self. The
spirituality and consciousness that I cherished so much
weren't being expressed at work anymore. Somewhere
along the way, it had diminished—not so much that
I noticed it happening, but gradually, like water leaking
out of a small hole in a bucket.*

*I started to feel that I was keeping my spirituality in the
closet. And my "feelings" were quite literally physical—at
night, a mysterious discomfort would surge in my abdo-
men. That discomfort led me down a path of discovery, as
I searched for what might be causing it. After seeing dozens
of conventional medical, integrative, and naturopathic
doctors with no relief, I knew I needed a break to figure
things out.*

I talked with my very understanding boss, who said, "Take a few months to decide what you need." It was a gift—a gift of space. It allowed me to take an inventory of myself, discover what was causing my pain, and learn what I really needed—physically and mentally and spiritually.

By the time my sabbatical was over, I knew I wasn't someone who could or would compartmentalize. One of my defining characteristics is my ability to bring my entire presence to everything. That included, notably, a safe place to bring spirituality into what I did every day. I wanted that opportunity for myself, and I wanted to offer that to others. And I never knew how much I needed that until I leaped.

Ultimately, I would leave my "ideal" career as a C-level executive at a massive company for a more authentic entrepreneurial path as an executive coach, spiritual teacher, and business strategist.

A Crisis of Purpose

JEFF'S STORY

My awakening, like Jennifer's, happened slowly, punctuated by a few acute moments of crisis and introspection. The most profound experience on my journey was losing my mother to cancer in 1999, when she was sixty-two.

Watching a parent fade away in front of my eyes had a massive impact on me. To this day, I can recall standing in a dark hospital room on a rainy January morning and hearing her doctor say, "There's nothing more we can do."

The doctor's words rang like a lightning bolt in my head. "In this day and age, we should never say those words about another human being," I thought. "We should always be able to do something." Feeling too old to go to medical school and too unprepared to become a research chemist, I looked for ways to engage more directly in saving lives.

My first stop was Salt Lake City, where I joined a small start-up and was tasked with building a team. Jennifer was the first person I hired. But while Jennifer found a decade-long career there, I was yearning for a way to directly help people like my mom.

That chance came several years later, when I left Campus Pipeline with enough management experience to lead a team at a large fundraising company. Here was an opportunity that seemed much more directly related to helping my mom—sure, I wasn't directly healing patients, but I was producing campaigns to raise money for the people who did. I met incredible people who shared the same passion for positive change as I.

That plan took an unexpected right turn, though, when the company I joined abruptly went bankrupt at the end of my second year there. And yet, that twist turned out to be a massive opportunity, too. With a committed team, two years of shared experience in the trenches, and plenty of passion, two colleagues and I struck out on our own. We started our own firm, Event 360, and spent over a decade creating large fundraising campaigns that raised hundreds of millions of dollars to fight cancer, AIDS, Alzheimer's, and mental illness.

I was finally "doing something." I was not only avenging my mother's death, but also helping prevent the deaths of thousands of others. It seemed like the culmination of everything I wanted and pursued.

And for a while, it really was—until one morning, nearly ten years later, when I received an early morning phone call from my sister while I was on the site of one of our fundraising events.

"Dad was just killed in a car accident today." She was crying so hard I almost couldn't understand her.

"Wait," I said. "Wait. What?"

My sister's voice was shaking. "Our dad, our only remaining parent, is dead."

My whole world collapsed in an instant. My career had been built on the idea that tragedy could be addressed, avoided, stopped. I could always do something.

One random car accident shattered that illusion.

I call the following year of my life "The Lost Year." I found it difficult to get interested in anything. For months, I couldn't sleep for more than a couple of hours a night, until a doctor prescribed an antidepressant—and after that, I couldn't focus. I found myself unable to concentrate on bigger projects or ideas.

I did my best to keep all of that to myself, although I'm sure my team noticed. I know my wife, Jeanie, did. My business partners were beyond understanding, but I could tell they were concerned about me and the company. I got by mainly by skating through the day, glossing over my feelings. I had become numb.

One morning in late spring, I recall waking up and going into the bathroom. As I brushed my teeth, I glanced in the mirror and caught my own reflection. I look tired. Haggard. My eyes were sunken and my skin was pale. I did not look like a "successful business owner coping with an unexpected loss" or whatever garbage I used to say to myself. I saw, simply, a sad boy.

I remember that one word came to me: "Orphan."

Yes, I was an adult. But with both of my parents gone, I had become an orphan, too.

I broke down in tears. Jeanie came in to see what was wrong. I said, "I need to get off these medications. I need to talk to someone. I need to deal with this."

In the year of healing that followed, I began to examine everything—my behavior, my faults, my accomplishments, and my work. I started to realize that the most recent part of my career, while so compelling, had been self-centered in a way. Through fundraising, I had really been driven by trying to paper over my own grief, rather than address the grief of others.

It was time to address that selfishness. It was time to learn how to truly serve.

Toward Co-Leadership

It was around this time, in 2015, that we both found ourselves participating in a mastermind retreat suggested by David Berry, a close mutual friend.

We spent two days sharing our paths, our accomplishments, our businesses, and our questions in the crisp, springtime mountain air of Park City. At seven thousand feet, the majestic vistas all around us inspired us to share our biggest visions, too. As we did, we were struck by how many similarities there were in our stories. The two of us could relate to the idea of doing *good* work that somehow didn't feel *great*. We could relate to the pull of doing something financially rewarding, and the tension between that and the things that felt spiritually rewarding. And we could relate to the desire to bridge that gap, in our own lives and for others.

By the end of the session, we could both feel the comfort and exhilaration of reconnecting with a kindred spirit. There was energy, life force, and excitement about the possibility of merging our efforts. The idea that we both didn't need to go it alone was refreshing and curious. There was a momentum that pulled us forward, leading to us combining our missions and companies.

So, we began one of our greatest and most challenging journeys—charting out a company that would help foster conscious leadership. It would help organizations and individuals find and act on purpose. It would help people feel and see they were enough. It would help teams and companies do good and well in the world. And those basics are what became Plenty.

We learned to dance. We stepped on each other's toes. We were each used to being *the* leader—so we had to learn to share space. We each had a big vision, and we had to learn that simply adding our two visions together wasn't cooperation—it was confusion. We had to learn to simplify. We had to learn to find what our ideas had in common, and distill those ideas down to a strong, shared core.

We both had to learn not to interrupt each other when we were listening—and to be more concise when we were speaking. We got hurt feelings when one of us would talk too much and not let the other in. We learned to deeply listen. Jen got better at holding space and breathing while Jeff spoke; Jeff worked on not interrupting her ideas with his own. We learned to share our perspectives and positions respectfully. When harmonious collaboration gave way to heated debate and defensiveness, as it tends to do in life, we used a hand signal to stop the conversation and take a time-out to create space.

We were each used to having a large team to help us get things done, so we had to learn to divvy up duties between ourselves, from time to time. We learned to share the credit—and the work.

We learned the power of compromise. We co-created. We practiced what we were teaching. We argued and closed the distance. We set intentions. We aligned and aligned and aligned.

Co-leadership has been one of the hardest and most rewarding things we've ever done.

Reaching Upward

Our personal and professional histories revealed quite a lot to us about how valuable each ring of growth can be—and how every tree must change through the seasons to maintain that growth. If you didn't know anything about a maple tree and saw one in December, standing stark and bare, you would think it was dead. But of course, it isn't—that dormant period is the preparation for new leaves in May. In a similar way, as we came together to create Plenty, we found that respect for change became central to our own evolution.

It's interesting. When we coach teams of people, we often hear a complaint that their organization "moves too fast." We'll hear, "There's too much change." We'll hear, "There's never any stability."

But without exception, when we coach the chief executives, creators, and entrepreneurs who lead those teams, *every single time* we hear, "Our biggest risk is that most of our people don't understand the need for change." The successful executives don't shield their employees from change—they see that their role is to *facilitate* it.

As a founder or top executive, you learn that you must be comfortable with people being uncomfortable, because change is what fosters growth. A lack of change isn't stability. It's stagnation. And the two of us, as serial founders and entrepreneurs, are no different from the founders and CEOs we coach: our role is to embrace change to facilitate growth.

That doesn't mean everyone else is going to be ready and willing, however. The eighteen months after we decided to work together were the most difficult of our careers. After our decision to work together, we had to merge two different business entities with existing brands, clients, and team members. We had to find a way to ramp down the traditional, transactional, revenue-driven, "bill for expertise" framework of consulting. We had to lay the groundwork for a firm that offered coaching rather than silver-bullet answers, that focused on the process as much as any product, that helped clients find their own wisdom rather than pedaling ours. And we had to be upfront about our values and ethos.

Our team was resistant at times, interested at others, curious sometimes, and occasionally combative. And who could blame them? They had signed up for something different. A few times we had to make some tough choices; other times, team members chose to leave the company on their own. And a few times, we took the wrong kind of work, until we got clearer about who we were and what we wanted.

There were fits and starts, accomplishments and setbacks, and looking back, we can see the growth rings in Plenty over time. We changed our public positioning. Embraced meditation and mindfulness in business before there were twenty apps for it. Branded our services, including Lantern, our leadership retreat, and the foundation of this book. Built out our private retreat center, HeartSpace, in Park City.

We followed our path—sometimes confidently, sometimes tentatively—and created the life we imagined for ourselves and others.

PRACTICE POINTS

Reflecting on Your Growth

Imagine you are a tree. You have several rings that have formed throughout out the years, all signifying your leaps, your courage, and your choices. Reflect on the major events or experiences that have shaped you into the being you are today.

- What have they taught you?

- Can you give thanks for them?

Or, take out a blank piece of paper or canvas. Draw your winding road from birth to now.

- Where were there twists and turns?

- What experiences changed the course of your path?

- How did you respond?

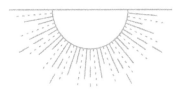

CHAPTER 3

What Is Conscious Leadership?

Have you ever told yourself, "If I can just make it through this week, I'll relax all weekend"?

It's all well and good to look forward to the weekend. But this is tricky. The thing is, "pushing through the week" can easily become "pushing through life." As humans, we're really good at "pushing through." We convince ourselves that the goal of life is to make it through to the weekend so that we can relish in the fruits of our labors. We forget that *actually being fulfilled by our labors* is even possible.

The months pass, the years add up, and suddenly you can find yourself five, ten, twenty years later doing something you *like* a lot at the expense of pursuing what you really *love*.

In his wonderful book *Illusions: The Adventures of a Reluctant Messiah*, Richard Bach wrote, "You are never given a wish without also being given the power to make it true."[1] We've come to believe passionately in this wisdom. The yearnings and impulses that we often dismiss are our heart's way of tapping us on the shoulder to remind us that our dreams are still in the room.

---

1 Richard Bach, *Illusions: The Adventures of a Reluctant Messiah* (New York: Dell Publishing, 1977).

We believe, too, that there's a cost for ignoring the tap. The more we ignore it, the louder it gets, and the more we have to use other tools to drown it out. You can probably list some of the tools: overwork, hollow relationships, alcohol, food, denial.

Note that not every wish is granted in the form we hope or expect it will be. The Divine works in mysterious ways that often don't make sense to our logical minds. But that doesn't mean you can't give yourself permission to wish, dream, and listen for the tap of the Divine on your shoulder. What does your heart yearn for?

The Path of Conscious Leadership

We're pointing you to a different way of thinking about leadership. Traditional leadership challenges primarily revolve around trying to keep a team motivated to accomplish a shared task. Facing those challenges requires a set of skills that can be incredibly daunting—and rewarding—to master. We don't want to diminish the value of this kind of leadership. It's critically important.

However, conscious leadership has a deeper connotation. This way of leading centers around becoming aware of and honest about *who you really are.*

Whereas traditional leadership is about understanding how to motivate others, conscious leadership is about learning to understand *yourself* and becoming your own motivation.

Whereas traditional leadership involves expressing yourself to others, conscious leadership involves becoming your *own* full expression.

Conscious leadership has three basic components:

- The call to be aware.

- The choice to be aligned.

- The invitation to be intentional.

Awareness:
The First Component of Conscious Leadership

What are you aware of right now?

Take your eyes off the page and look around. What do you see? What do you hear? Maybe you see the furniture in your living room or the books lining your office. Maybe you hear traffic outside or the sound of kids playing in the other room.

Now, can you bring awareness to what you feel? Do you feel happy? Restless? Content? Uncertain? Grateful? Stressed?

Where do you feel it? In your stomach? Your chest? Your throat?

As you start to tune into your awareness, notice your thoughts. Is your mind present with what's around you? Or are you getting distracted, perhaps thinking about what you need to do after you put down this book?

Notice how you feel answering these questions. Are they interesting to you? Do you find yourself curious about them? Is your mood a bit higher as you read these words?

Or does this activity feel like busywork? Too pedantic, too trite, too boring? Do you find yourself annoyed or trying to rush ahead to the next page to get to something more interesting?

Now go one level deeper. Can you notice *who* is noticing? In other words, how are you able to know if you're interested or distracted, curious or annoyed? That seems odd, right? After all, you are lost in thought! How can you identify what you're thinking if you are the one thinking it?

How is it that you can sometimes step out of your feelings and notice them like a neutral observer?

As humans, we can get so stressed that we can only see the huge pile of work in front of us. Yet at other times, we can take half a step back, detach, and say, "Wow, I am having feelings of stress."

We can get so angry with another person that all we can do is lash out at them. Or we can get a tiny bit of space to say, "I'm feeling angry with you, so I need to go outside and cool off before I say something I'll regret."

Sometimes, we can be so full of joy that we laugh and play and get lost in the moment. Other times, we have enough awareness of that joy to say, "I'm so grateful for this moment."

Conscious leadership starts with awareness. "Awareness" is partly about being observant—about creating a bit of space between our thoughts and *what we think of our thoughts*. That's the noticing we've started to practice these last few pages.

At Plenty, we talk about the practice of awareness as "seeing what is." What we mean is seeing situations at their base level, stripped of personal commentary. There's a difference between "My partner has left me, and so once again I've learned I'm totally unlovable" and "My relationship has ended." There's a difference between "I'm totally broke, a mess financially, and

I'll never work again" and "Currently I have one month of pay in my bank account."

Awareness involves taking an objective look at your situation and the commentary you apply to it. Sometimes, our own commentary actively works against our ability to see what is true.

As you read the rest of this chapter and this book, pay attention to your thoughts. What ideas spark your interest? What ideas turn you off? What do you notice as you think about them?

Expansion and Contraction

As you develop your capacity for greater awareness, you'll improve your relationship to expansion and contraction—a key characteristic of the difference between what you like and what you don't.

For many of us, when we are expanded by something, we open up, we become interested, and we are ready for more. We have generally positive feelings. We are curious. We want to learn more. We naturally lean in.

On the other hand, when we're contracted by something, we may find ourselves pulling back. We pause. We procrastinate. Sometimes, we become skeptical. We turn off. We find it hard to pay attention, or at times actively disengage from whatever is contracting us.

How do you feel when you are expanded? How do you feel when you are contracted?

You often can notice expansion and contraction in body language. Have you ever started a meeting by sharing an idea you liked, only to look around to see everyone staring at you with crossed arms? That's contraction. When someone is contracted by a thought, idea, or conversation, they usually cross their arms. They may step backward. They likely tense up. They may frown or look away.

Expansion, on the other hand, often looks like enthusiasm. Someone who is expanded looks more excited. The tone of their voice gets higher and faster. They may start talking with their hands. They will physically lean into the conversation. When Jennifer is expanded, she gets red in the face and neck. Jeff holds onto his coffee cup a bit tighter because Jen's hands will go flying as she talks!

A key component of awareness is observing what expands and contracts you. What lights you up? Think about scanning your calendar in the morning. What meetings or activities make you smile when you see them? What makes you show up early for work?

Similarly, what appointments and tasks cause you to roll your eyes and groan? When do you get a pit in your stomach? What do you find yourself procrastinating on?

These are all cues to what expands you and what contracts you. These cues open you to a new level of awareness.

The problem is, you may be like so many leaders who have gotten good at *ignoring* these cues to get things done. There's nothing wrong with doing work—in fact, we believe the Universe is always asking each of us, every day, to play a part in creating our own future. Unfortunately, many of us have come to equate "work" with "difficulty" or even "misery." We can get so good at focusing on the *effort* that we become numb to the cues our own body and soul are giving us about what we really *like* to do.

To become a conscious leader, you are asked to listen to your full self. Conscious leadership calls you into an honest awareness—noticing what works for you and what doesn't, observing where you lean in and where you lean out, and listening to your own instincts and the cues around you. Being honest about what expands and contracts you is the first step to a more fulfilling life.

More Than Observation

When we talk about awareness, we mean more than observing your reactions to what is happening around you. We also mean becoming aware of your commentary about life—the way you speak to yourself each moment of the day.

Do you speak to yourself as you would your best friend? Or your worst enemy?

We'll talk more about how to create space between yourself and your thoughts in the coming chapters. For now, we want to point you to the idea that at times, you can be lost in your thoughts—but at other times, you can almost rise beyond them as a neutral observer, so you can see *how* you are thinking.

That's a powerful realization: You are not your thoughts. You are something more. And that realization is the call to become more deeply aware.

Running into the Glass Wall

Tim is one of our all-time favorite clients. An executive at a large company in the food industry, Tim is energetic, passionate, and engaging. He wears his emotions on his sleeve, puts his whole being into his work, and brightens up every room he's in.

Tim has hired Plenty three or four times to help him create purpose-driven strategies for various brands he's led. Working with him, our team has traveled across North America, met dozens of other incredible leaders and change-makers, helped grow his business by tens of millions of dollars in revenue, and raised millions of dollars for their nonprofit partners. We love it.

When we first met Tim, though, he was really stressed. As you may know all too well from your own professional experience, stress is sometimes the trade-off for investing your whole self in your work—sometimes you don't know where the work stops and the "you" begins.

The first time we collaborated with Tim, we were working to launch a new initiative for a growing brand. Our team was on-site for a multiday series of meetings with Tim and his team. The schedule was so tight that Tim was running concurrent meetings in separate rooms. He'd introduce us to one team, and we'd start the strategy session while Tim would bounce out to another room to take part in different discussions.

The pace was fast, exciting, and honestly, totally unsustainable—like riding a rickety bike down a dirt mountain path and thinking, "Oh boy, this is going to topple over any second." We had the sense that everyone, while engaged, was also getting fried.

We were planning to pull Tim aside to say, "Hey, we think we need to slow down for a bit to let everyone really understand what we're all trying to create here." The trick was, how would we even get a moment to pull him out of his work, given his incredible pace?

On a short break, we were talking through our best opportunities to pull him aside. We'll never forget what happened next, while we were standing outside of the conference room in their headquarters—one of those sleek, modern offices with full-length glass doors and walls to help create openness and transparency.

Lost in thought, Tim walked right by us without stopping. As we watched, he walked, full speed, directly into a closed glass door. *Thonk*! We must admit it was pretty funny to witness! But he also looked like he was going to have one heck of a bruise. We weren't sure whether to laugh or run to help as his forehead bounced off the glass.

We did both. By the time we got to his side, Tim, to his credit, had gotten the message. He smiled and said, "Time to become more aware of my surroundings."

Being Here Now

When the Divine Muse gives you a sign this good, you use it! And we have used the story five or six dozen times, sometimes with Tim in the room. His experience is such a great lesson about what we mean by awareness.

Awareness doesn't mean being lost in thought. It's the opposite. It means understanding that you are not your thoughts. Your thoughts come and go, moving like clouds across the sky, but you are the sun, watching from above the clouds.

Conscious leadership is about cultivating this awareness. Awareness includes being present to whatever you are doing in the moment. Awareness means listening to your body's sensations. Awareness means not getting so lost in your stresses, fears, dreams, and desires that you find yourself running into walls—metaphorically or literally.

Cultivating awareness also means being present to what you *really* want. It means being tuned in to what expands you and what contracts you, and how those two things change over time. For many leaders, awakening to this consciousness can be liberating—and scary. After all, many of us have gotten where we are precisely by denying or delaying what we really want! But this new way forward starts with leaning into those yearnings, instead of out.

Awareness Isn't Always Easy

Maybe there's a reason many of us get good at denying what we truly want, ignoring our soul's deepest callings, and settling for less. Awareness isn't always easy. It isn't always pleasurable to be conscious of your emotions, particularly your less-than-flattering ones. When you become more aware of your emotions, you realize that you harbor many that are petty, childish, and just plain silly.

JEFF'S STORY:

A few years ago, I served as Plenty's consultant to a group of business CEOs who were assembling a peer group for ongoing mentorship. I knew the members, so I volunteered to facilitate a few sessions to help them get clear about the kind of support they wanted to create for one another.

By the second or third planning meeting, I was starting to get attached to the group—and to the idea of leading it. The discussion turned to whom to hire as the facilitator. I grew increasingly agitated as the members listed the requirements for their ideal candidate. Experienced. Professional. Thoughtful. I found myself standing up during the discussion, pacing the room. Finally, my pride couldn't take it and I heard myself almost cry out, red in the face: "But this is exactly what we do at Plenty!"

Look at me!

It wasn't my most graceful moment, for sure.

Later, I was fortunate that one of my mentors in the room pulled me aside. "Hey Jeff," he said, "you may want to play it cool on your role here. Let the group go through its paces, and if you're the right fit, it will come back to you." Under his feedback, I heard a more powerful message: "The more you have to tell us why you are the perfect fit, the less we believe you."

I had an uncomfortable awareness of how attached and insecure I had become (feelings that often go together for me). That awareness was hard to take, but it was powerful. And helpful. I pulled back, encouraged them to interview candidates on the market, and said I'd volunteer to help until they found someone. Six months later, the group leadership came back and said, "We've interviewed a few different people and we think we found the right person— it's you."

JEN'S STORY:

Last year, as one of four volunteer parents coaching my daughter's seventh grade lacrosse league, I was struggling to find my role. I was comfortable being the head coach, since I had served in that position for over twenty-five years. But I was still working to become comfortable assisting, as my limited availability prevented me from taking on the responsibility of creating every practice plan and leading each practice.

As a person innately wired for leadership, I was being challenged on both a subtle and not-so-subtle level. Over several practices, I could feel a tension build between what I wanted to lean into, what was possible, and what was wanted by others. Among all the coaches, I had the most coaching and playing experience. But it didn't seem like the other coaches saw or valued that. I soon found myself in a power struggle with one of the them. I felt personally dismissed as we worked our way through determining responsibility for tasks. Unconsciously, I found myself needing to prove my knowledge, and I became aware of a lot of interference between what I instinctually wanted to share and a worry that I would be judged if I did. I discovered that I was defending my perspective and experience more than I needed or wanted to, which led me to want to withdraw from helping altogether. But the idea of not coaching my daughter and participating in the sport I had brought to the state was crushing.

Suddenly, I had a breakthrough: the insight that my feelings had nothing to do with any of the other coaches. They

*had to do with me! I was taking things way too personally.
I was projecting an inner desire to be seen and respected by
others, rather than trusting and honoring myself.*

*The moment I had this awareness, the desire to be seen
in a certain way lost its grip on me, and I showed up to
practice with more peace and space. I went with the flow.
I led when I felt called to and assisted when that role was
needed. My love of the sport and coaching returned, and
I reconnected with my intention in being there in the first
place: to serve, inspire, and lead.*

We've both had lots and lots of experience in being uncomfortable with our own awareness. But leaning into that awareness, instead of damping it down, has opened us up to massive growth. It's taught us that we don't need to be afraid of our dreams, and we don't need to be ashamed of our faults. The more we practice being aware of what we want, how we act, and how we are reacting, the clearer we get on who and how we want to be.

When you practice taking an inventory of how you truly feel, you awaken your soul to the possibility of a life more aligned to your purpose.

Alignment:
The Second Component of Conscious Leadership

Becoming aware in this multidimensional way can feel like a new frontier for many leaders. And like all frontiers, it brings opportunities and challenges. The biggest opportunity is the chance to live a life of your choosing. The challenge, often, is what to do if you suddenly become aware that the life you're living isn't the one you want to choose anymore.

That takes us to the second part of conscious leadership: the choice to be aligned.

What Is Alignment?

Alignment is living in accordance with what expands you. It means acting on your awareness—choosing what works for you and what doesn't.

For example, think of this scenario: You wake up every day with a pit in your stomach. It's been happening now for weeks—sometimes only on certain days, but more and more, you feel a bit off in the morning. For a while, you brush it off. You notice that having a good meal, seeing a movie, or going for a night out takes your mind off it.

After a few months, you wake up feeling great on a Saturday morning. Suddenly it hits you: you never have a pit in your stomach on the weekends. Bingo! That's the start of awareness.

Now, if you brush off that realization, you're back where you started. But let's say you don't. Let's say you step further into what you just realized. You might realize, "I used to wake up eager to go to work, but since our bigger competitor acquired us, I've grown increasingly overworked." Or you might realize, "I used to love the people I worked with, but since the pandemic, we're all working from home, and my job has become too impersonal."

Now you're starting to build a different understanding of yourself. You're using your awareness to create further understanding. You're not ignoring it or medicating it out. You're in the process of inquiry. We'll expand on some tools to help you do that in the next several chapters.

Eventually, you'll come to some conclusions. Note there's no "right" solution—*there's only what's right for you, right now.* Maybe what's right is to quit the company because it just doesn't fit anymore. But maybe what you need is just to start going to the in-person office again. Or to talk to your boss about hiring additional staff to help with the workload.

Ultimately, this awareness leads you to some choice points. *Alignment is making the choice.* Remember, you're not given a wish (awareness) without the power to make it true (choice). You may have to work for it, however—and the work is alignment. Alignment is mustering the courage to trust your instincts instead of talking yourself out of them.

What do you have to do to become more aligned with who you are?

- Let go of fear that you won't find a job.

- Trust in your abilities.

- Release your attachment to the idea that you're not meant to be happy.

- Believe there's more out there for you.

- Stop identifying as the one who "has it all together" and trust people will love you, messiness and all.

And so forth—whatever you're doing, you probably need to extend more trust in order to step more fully into what your awareness is telling you that you want.

Alignment is about making those choices.

Awareness Isn't Enough

There's a myth that usually crops up when we start talking about alignment. The myth is that once we understand what we want, we simply need to "put it out there" and the Universe—or God or Spirit or the Divine—will come to our assistance. The misguided thinking is that our role is to simply be aware and set intention, and the rest will take care of itself.

We believe strongly in the power of intention and in the power of the Divine. We'll talk about both in a lot of detail later in the book. But the unfortunate truth we've learned is that, as humans, we don't get to pick how the Universe works. *Often, the way the Universe helps us act is by presenting us with the very obstacles we wish it would take away.*

Can you think of a time in your life when something unexpected, unwanted, and unappreciated became the stimulus for incredible growth? Maybe your employer went suddenly bankrupt, leaving you with no more excuses to delay the entrepreneurial venture you'd always dreamed about. Maybe a car wreck finally forced you to slow down, creating the sabbatical you needed (though not in the way you would have chosen). Maybe your spouse left you, forcing you to finally confront your unwillingness to become vulnerable or your need to stop seeking validation from others.

These are the Mack Truck moments we talked about earlier—extreme cases of what we would call *universal intervention*.

But similar interventions are happening all throughout the day. Often, they are so subtle we don't notice them. The inclination to reach out to an old friend. The sudden realization that you can solve a problem in a way you hadn't thought of previously. A new idea that comes to you after a run. An unexpected financial gift someone grants you. As you increase your awareness, you'll notice these interventions happening all the time.

Now you need to decide what to do with them.

In no way, shape, or form are we trying to say that conscious leadership is about being passive. There's *effort* that's going to be required from you. In fact, there's a second sentence to the Richard Bach quote we mentioned earlier. His full passage is, "You are never given a wish without also being given the power to make it true. You may have to work for it, however."[2]

You will have to play a part.

"But wait, Jennifer and Jeff," you might be thinking. "You said in the earlier section that I needed to let go of pushing, striving, and working."

What we're pointing to is a different way of thinking about the work that's being asked of you. What if "doing the work" meant building the awareness, courage, stamina, and resilience to *follow* your callings, instead of honing your ability to ignore, delay, or deny them?

---

2 Richard Bach, *Illusions: The Adventures of a Reluctant Messiah* (New York: Dell Publishing, 1977).

In other words, what if, instead of the old paradigm of working hard to get what you *think* you want, you could instead embrace a new paradigm of first doing the work to *understand* what you truly *love*, and then follow the best, easiest, and most fulfilling path to it? That's conscious leadership.

Said another way, conscious leadership isn't about waiting for the Universe to take you where you want to go. *Conscious leadership is about walking in the direction the Universe is pointing to.* The ability to see that pointing is awareness. The choice to start walking is alignment.

Leaving the Trojan Horse Behind

At Plenty, we seldom write sales proposals that we don't close. That's not because we're incredible salespeople or fantastic pitch artists. Instead, it's because we've gotten very aware of what we want to do and have aligned our marketing around it.

When interested clients look at our website, they get a clear idea of how we think and act. Our hearts are on our sleeves. Plenty's tagline is "Our purpose is to help you find yours"—and we list our competencies as conscious leadership, conscious business strategy, conscious culture, and spiritual growth. Our podcast and blog regularly feature stories and interviews about living a life of purpose, connecting with spirit, the power of the heart, and why passion is at the center of business.

In other words, we're open about who we are. And we're open about the fact that our way isn't for everyone. Potential clients who don't resonate with our way of thinking rarely call us. We use our website to both attract people who are interested and weed out those who aren't.

The thing is, we didn't always market ourselves this way. Seven or eight years ago, we were advised that business leaders didn't want to talk about passion and purpose, emotions and spirituality. Our own team told us, "Don't be too touchy-feely." We heard that "meditation is personal, not professional."

Our employees and our agencies seemed to be certain about this, so we took a marketing approach that internally we called the Trojan Horse. We'd position ourselves as a traditional consulting agency, and when we surfaced the inevitable cultural, self-esteem, and wellbeing issues that underpin every strategic problem, we'd then wheel out our larger toolset around conscious leadership.

It worked, kind of. The Trojan Horse approach became a surprise bonus when we worked with high-functioning teams. High-functioning teams have a shared set of values, are generally willing to communicate openly, and have moved past power struggles and the individual insecurities that cause them.

We've learned that most issues that get in the way of high-functioning teams are alignment issues. In other words, the team *knows* what the problems are, but they can't agree on how to solve them. With those teams, our Trojan Horse approach worked great. Once we'd begun to explore issues with a high-functioning team, it would become clear that to align on a shared solution, everyone would have to be willing to have honest discussions about what was working, what wasn't, and why.

Self-aware teams love conversations like that—they are frustrated that they can't solve the problems they see, and they jump at the chance to have a conscious conversation about what's really going on and what the choices are. They realize, "Oh, we thought we were hiring a traditional consulting group, but you brought so much more to the table." We can look back at the references we have from our first few years of growth and see many testimonials like that. "It was so much more than I thought it would be."

But the Trojan Horse approach failed miserably with teams that weren't functioning well. Low-functioning teams can't jump right to alignment. Members hide their feelings, don't feel safe enough to share, backstab one another, work according to hidden agendas, build silos, and keep score. Those kinds of behaviors often have their roots in personal insecurities. The personal insecurities create barriers to real, open conversation.

So, we'd go into these environments thinking the teams would want to address the personal thinking underlying their group dynamics. Nope. We'd run into a brick wall, time and time again. We'd hear, "You're way out of scope. Stay in your lane. We hired Plenty to help us with our strategy—that's it. We don't want to do all this personal stuff." Some of the fiascos were quite spectacular! Once, we had a founder almost end a four-day strategy retreat after the first day; another time, we presided over a roundtable that devolved into a name-calling session. We lost a few large clients primarily because they were the wrong clients for us in the first place. We hadn't been willing to make the conscious choice to align our marketing with our own awareness of what we loved to do. It hurt our pride—and our pocketbook.

We did some big soul-searching. We decided to own who we were and who we wanted to be. We chose to let go of the team members who weren't interested in talking about conscious leadership, spirit, purpose, and possibility. We scrapped the Trojan Horse and put our ethos right on the front page of our site. We said "no" to sales calls and request-for-proposals that didn't fit anymore. We turned away business and fell out of pace with our old competitors as we staked out new territory for ourselves.

We had to go through our own decision to align our work with our awareness.

It was a bit scary to write, "We help conscious leaders and businesses grow" at the top of our home page and at the bottom of every email. But we intentionally chose those terms because they resonated with us and we felt they openly described how we think. And you know what? After a while, we started to notice that the sales inquiries we were getting were a whole lot more interesting—and more relevant.

We started to hear things like, "We looked at your website a year ago and decided to go with a company that seemed like a more traditional strategy firm. A year and $250,000 later, we're no further along. We need to try something different. Would you be willing to talk?" We heard statements like this so often that we started to use that language on our site: "If you want to make a difference in the world, you need a different kind of consultant."

We realized that the more we shared our dream of a world of purpose and consciousness, the more we'd attract the people who wanted that, too. Once we became aware of what we wanted and aligned our language with it, everything got easier.

Beyond Analysis Paralysis

Once you start to experiment with awareness, you're likely to find many choices and places where you can become more aligned. The book is in part about helping you make those choices. To start, we'll simply repeat the basic decision-making rule we wrote earlier:

There's only what's right for you, right now.

It's a powerful idea, and one we'll explore more deeply in the following chapters.

Intention:
The Third Component of Conscious Leadership

Intention is the ongoing commitment to making continual choices based on your awareness.

We use the idea of intention a lot in our work because it is a powerful driver of transformation. We've found that most leaders are very familiar with goals, but they aren't as sure about what is meant by "intention."

Intentions are related to goals, but different. At Plenty, this is how we distinguish the two: goals denote what you hope to *achieve* with your life, while intentions denote how you hope to *be* as you live those achievements.

Most of us are taught a lot about goals as we grow up: I'm going to achieve this, or I'm going to do that. Goals can be very useful because they can help us channel our choices and focus our efforts. Goals can help us walk with purpose instead of stumbling down the path.

But goals are only a part of the story. They focus on outcomes. Intentions, on the other hand, are based on inputs—what you want to *bring* to the process. *If goals describe what you hope to find at the end of the path, intentions describe how you'd like to feel as you start walking.*

In our achievement-oriented world, goals garner most of the publicity. But as we grow more aware and aligned, intentions become much more powerful. Outcomes, in many situations, are beyond our control. Intentions, however, are always our own. We can always determine how we want to be, regardless of what happens around us. And goals, ironically, can sometimes work against our own desires. Goals can take us away from the present, shifting our minds to always live in search of some supposedly better future state. Intentions bring us back to the now, encouraging us to create that future in every moment.

The Power of Intention

Intentions powerfully set the frame for our experience, reinforcing our awareness and alignment. Imagine two people who share the same goal: to run their first marathon in under five hours. Now consider the impact of intention: One person intends to be the fastest runner in their age group. The other person sets the intention to have fun and meet new people while training.

The goal is the same—run a marathon in under five hours. But can you see how the different intentions may create very different experiences? One experience might be joyful and expansive, no matter how the runner's time turns out. The other experience might be tedious and disappointing if the desired outcome isn't achieved.

As a quick exercise, try supplementing your goals with some intentions, or perhaps try replacing your goals altogether. Instead of saying, "I want to lose ten pounds" (a common resolution after the holidays), try, "I show my own body respect every day in how I treat it and what I feed it." What would change?

Instead of saying, "This year, I finally want to find a better job" (a noble goal), what if you said, "I put my full heart into everything I do." How might that impact your satisfaction?

Instead of resolving to find a better relationship, what if you said, "I treat myself with gentleness and love and expect others to do the same." How would that focus your awareness and alignment on your own self-love? If you always treated yourself with respect, how might that change what kind of partner you attracted?

These are just examples. We don't assume to know what's best for you. Your intentions, like your goals, are your own. But we do believe that you're more incredible than you know. When you create this kind of framework for your intentions, you're more likely to live in a way that keeps you aware and aligned with how you'd like to be.

It may sound trite, but it isn't. In a single-minded focus on our goals, we can miss most of the journey. Intentions help us stay right here, in the present, where life can actually find us. *The wonder comes in the walking.*

Conscious leaders consider what they want to achieve. Goals are still important. But conscious leaders also ask a deeper question in the realm of intention: What do I want to *experience*?

Bringing It Together: The River

To describe the role of awareness, alignment, and intention—and to describe the journey of conscious leadership more generally—we use a metaphor that's become powerful for us. We talk about rafting down the river.

During the summer of 2020—when the world was still fairly locked down, everyone was doing their best to stay safe, and parents like us were trying to find ways to occupy stir-crazy kids—both of our families, separately, decided to take river-rafting trips.

The Mulhollands took a week-long guided trip down the Salmon River in Idaho. The Shucks went to the Smokey Mountains to raft the Pigeon Forge and the Nantahala.

We both came back amazed by the journeys we had experienced, and ever since, we've shared the river metaphor with every Lantern retreat class we've held. It's the most succinct way we've found to describe conscious leadership. It offers us a straightforward way to visualize the ideas of awareness, alignment, and intention.

The river flows, quickly in some places and slowly in others, according to its own designs. Where the river flows, the river goes, and only the river knows. Whether you're on the river or staring at it from the shore, you can look far in each direction, but you can't see its start or its end. The river stretches far into the distance both in front of and behind you.

You can push against the current if you want, and perhaps if the current is slow enough, you can make some progress upstream. But you'll never out-force the river. Sooner or later, you'll realize it is faster to paddle with the current.

In some places, the current will take you where it wants, no matter how you steer or where you paddle. In other places, you can maneuver yourself on the current, taking advantage of its flow. You can learn to spot the flow and ease into it, just like you can learn to see the rapids and eddies if you are paying attention.

When you aren't paying attention, you risk ending up far off course, or worse, injuring yourself or others. When you are paying attention, you find you can make vast amounts of progress, covering miles at a speed you didn't think was possible.

It's a one-person raft, this vessel we're each sitting in—and yet, it's not a solo journey. There are other rafts along the river—some further ahead, some a bit behind, some catching the flow, some drifting in circles, but all generally moving with the current, heading the same direction.

You can choose to stand on the shore if you want, and that will keep you safe and dry—but it won't get you anywhere. You have to get on the water.

You can throw your paddle away if you want, giving away your agency and hoping for the best—but that will likely leave you frustrated and dashed against the rocks. If you want to arrive somewhere specific, you have to pick up your paddle and steer.

You can choose to be angry or happy, sad or grateful, about the fact that you're sitting in a small raft on a large, flowing river—your choice of mood won't impact the river at all. But your mood will impact your journey a great deal.

The river is the journey of conscious leadership. We're called to be *aware*. We're called to get on the water—to understand that life itself is the great invitation. We're not meant to stay dry. We're meant to wake up, climb aboard, and sometimes get wet.

We're called to *align* ourselves—to pick up our paddles and steer. We're not meant to ride like a stick on the surface, or we wouldn't have been given feelings and intellect and talent and dreams. That doesn't mean we get to choose where the river goes, or that paddling against the current will get us very far. It only means that we're all given a choice to paddle or not, to do our best to find the current and ride with it.

And we're called to be *intentional*. We're called to bring awareness to our emotions, thoughts, and feelings, and align them with the dreams we feel in our hearts. The river takes us mainly where it wants, and so the grand experiment is to decide how we'll relate to that. Will we go with the flow? Will we ride the current? Will we be grateful? Will we be resentful? Will we use the gifts we have? Will we complain about the gifts we don't? It's ours to decide.

It's not always easy. It's not always safe. And that is what makes the journey on the river so rewarding.

Lighting Your Way

We've spent this chapter exploring three components of conscious leadership:

- The call to be aware.

- The choice to be aligned.

- The invitation to be intentional.

From our own experience, we know it is one thing to understand the idea of conscious leadership. It's something else entirely to try to *practice* awareness, alignment, and intentionality every day.

"Practice" is a key word, because just like the journey on the river, the journey of conscious leadership has waypoints, but it doesn't ever end. Philosopher Richard Rohr wrote, "I have prayed for years for one good humiliation a day."[3] What he means, in part, is that the feeling of humility is his sign that he is still growing and learning, testing the edges of his ego and awareness.

It's an ongoing journey—sometimes fulfilling, sometimes frightening, sometimes joyful, sometimes dark and mysterious. To help with your journey of practice, we've outlined Four Lights of Conscious Leadership to help guide your way as you head down the river. We teach these at our retreats and in our engagements with leaders just like you.

---

3 Richard Rohr, *Falling Upward: A Spirituality for the Two Halves of Life* (San Francisco: Jossey-Bass, 2011).

Over the next four chapters, we'll explore each of these Lights in turn, and help you guide your own path to greater awareness, alignment, and intention.

I.   You Are Light

II. Your Light Is Always On

III. You Only Have To See What Is Right in Front of You

IV. There Is a Larger Light Guiding You

PRACTICE POINTS

Practicing Awareness,

Alignment, and Intention

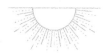

Increasing Your Awareness

"Seeing what is" is a powerful approach to observe where we are and where we want to be. Understanding how others perceive us, as well as how we perceive ourselves and our natural personality traits, tendencies, leanings, and longings, can all help increase our self-awareness. Assessments are one of our favorite tools for getting to better know our light, our style, and our unique makeup.

We value assessments so much that we've created several ourselves. Here are a few that can help you become more aware of yourself.

1. **The Lantern Leadership Assessment.** This assessment is a tool we've created to help you see what kind of leader you are—and get clear on what kind of leader you'd like to be. We developed this assessment to help our clients and retreat attendees better understand themselves, so they can better lead others. It has been taken by thousands of leaders from all industries and walks of life.

    The assessment measures your perceptions about your approach to conscious leadership. It is designed to help you understand your values and vision, your style, and your way. The questions are built on our Lantern Leadership Model, which is the foundation of this book and a framework that we use to coach leaders from all industries, at all levels, worldwide. Best of all, it's free. You can take it here: www.plentyconsulting .com/the-lantern-leadership-assessment.

2. **The Five Keys Assessment for Conscious Culture.** As you become more intentional as a conscious leader, you may find that you look for ways to bring more awareness, alignment, and intention into your workplace, too. Finding purpose is more important than ever. Your team members are just like you—over the last few years, many have had to rethink what they do every day and why they do it. More than ever, we're seeking deeper meaning and connection in our work and our lives. The Five Keys Assessment for Conscious Culture—or "the Five Keys" for short—is designed to help organizations clarify their vision and purpose to create more conscious, productive, and fulfilling cultures. In other words, we use it to help groups identify what really matters and why. Try it for yourself at www.plentyconsulting.com/ the-five-keys-assessment-for-conscious-culture.

3. **The Lumeria Wellbeing Assessment.** The path to being a more conscious leader runs directly through personal wellbeing. As you become more aware of what works and what doesn't, you naturally want to align with thoughts and habits that work better for

you. The Lumeria Wellbeing Assessment is designed to help you assess your connection to your innate health, vitality, and wellbeing and the relationship you currently have with your mind, body, and soul. We believe wellbeing is your natural state. You were designed to be healthy, happy, and whole—you only have to look at the intelligence behind your immune system, your incredible ability to heal, and your enduring capacity to feel better to see that there is an inherent state of wellbeing in your design. That said, we don't always feel that way. We get stressed, worried, and anxious. That's okay. That's the path of being human. This assessment is a step for you along that path. Take it for free at www.plentyconsulting.com/the-lumeria-wellbeing-assessment.

4. Another assessment we've used ourselves and with our teams is called the **Five Love Languages**. You may have already used it. We find that it has been an invaluable awareness tool to help us better understand how we naturally communicate, how we seek connection, and how we feel heard and seen. Dr. Gary Chapman first created the Five Love Languages Quiz to help people improve their relationships. It's been so widely used that he has adapted it for business, parenting, the military, and more. Check it out at 5lovelanguages.com.

5. The final assessment we recommend is called **Human Design**. Human Design blends your astrology, numerology, and more to give you a better understanding of our how you can use your body's

innate design for decision-making. It is calculated based on your birth date, time, and place. We've found it to be an incredibly rich, accurate, and deep awareness tool. You can take it here: www.myhuman design.com/get-your-chart/.

Practicing Alignment

Align Your Roles

Refer back to the list of roles you made in chapter 1. Are you aligned with the roles you play? In other words, are you intentional about where you shine your light? Here's a simple exercise to bring more awareness, alignment, and intentionality to the roles you play. Once you notice what roles are in alignment or out of alignment for you, you can then choose which ones you want to keep and which ones you don't.

1. First, review the list of all the roles you play—and if you didn't make one earlier, now is your chance! We all wear a variety of hats and spin a lot of plates. Allow yourself to think of all the roles you play in your personal and professional life. Again, note that we're not talking about "titles." Rather, we mean the roles you play within those titles. For example, you may fall under the title of "mother" to your children. The roles within that could range from coach, listener, and mentor to quarterback, dishwasher, and nagger. Some roles within each title are likely fulfilling, while others are probably draining. Other examples of roles we hear are things like partner, champion, trusted adviser,

listener, convener, get-it-doner, planner, confidant, creator, cleaner, pick-it-up-er, gardener, beautifier, IT support, musician, athlete, and so forth.

2. Once your list feels complete, take a blank page and draw a large T on it. Separate your page into two columns, "Aligned" and "Not Aligned." Under the Aligned column, list roles that harness your passions and your strengths. Under the Not Aligned column, include roles that you don't want to play anymore—or put differently, roles that are not aligned to your light. What do you notice? Are you ready to drop the roles that are not aligned to your light anymore? Can you delegate those roles to someone else in your family or on your team? Do you need to hire them out? Or have an honest conversation with your coworkers or family about who is doing what?

Practicing Intention Setting

1. **Speak your intention for the day, meeting, or month ahead.**

   As soon as your feet hit the floor after you've woken up, set the intention for how you want to feel at the end of the day. You can say it to yourself, verbalize it out loud, or write it down.

   At the top of your meeting agendas, write down your intention for the meeting. Share it with your meeting participants at the beginning of your discussion and ask them to help actualize it during the meeting.

Before you go for a walk with a friend or have a meaty conversation with a loved one, set your intention. How do you want to feel at the end of the exchange? Again, you can simply get clear inside your mind, or you can write it down.

2. **To clarify your intentions and help them come to life, write a manifestation letter.**

This is one of our favorite rituals to do on the winter solstice (on or around December 21st) each year, but you can do it any time of the year. Writing a manifestation letter is a wonderful way to start the year intentionally.

Set your sacred space. Find a quiet environment where you won't be disturbed. Arrange your setting with candles, music, lighting, and whatever else you need to be calm and present.

Gather a few pieces of paper, a pen, and an envelope. Date your letter one year in the future.

Close your eyes and take a few deep breaths.

To orient yourself, take a few moments to look back in time to see and feel what you experienced over the past year. Now, imagine it is a year from now. Imagine your hopes and dreams coming true. Imagine what you want to experience as if, with the snap of your fingers, you could manifest anything and any experience you desire—your heart's longing coming true. What do you experience? How do you feel? What do you accomplish? Feel yourself smiling from the inside out, as if everything has come true.

When you are ready, open your eyes, grab your pen, and write: "Dear [fill in your name], as I look back on the past year, I am so grateful for . . ." and write down all the things you are thankful for experiencing as if they have already occurred. Be as specific or as general as you want, allowing your heart and soul's longings to be known to you. Emphasize how you *feel*, for it is our feelings that create the vibrations we emit, and those vibrations attract what we experience.

Write until you feel complete—in other words, until you find a natural pause and feel you have written enough.

When you are finished, place your letter in an envelope and self-address it (put your name and address in the return address place as well). Seal the envelope and put it in a safe place where you will remember to retrieve it a year from now. Or, you can send it to us to keep safely for you: Plenty, Attn.: Manifestation Letter, 4343 Highway 224, Suite 203, Park City, Utah 84098. We will send it back to you a year later.

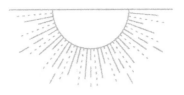

CHAPTER 4

The First Light
You Are Light

Saying that conscious leadership involves the call to be aware, the choice to be aligned, and the invitation to be intentional seems straightforward. But knowing how you'd like to be and *being* that way are two different things. How can we practice better awareness? How do we know when we're out of alignment? How do we remind ourselves to be intentional?

As we built our conscious leadership retreat, Lantern, those questions came up again and again. We realized we needed a short set of reminders to help our attendees practice awareness, alignment, and intentionality. The reminders also happened to be the core tenets of our own conscious leadership path.

Over time, these reminders coalesced into what we call the Four Lights of Conscious Leadership—or simply the Four Lights. Together, they form a set of guideposts—not exactly a set of things to do, but a set of reminders about how to practice being a conscious leader.

THE FOUR LIGHTS OF CONSCIOUS LEADERSHIP

I — YOU ARE LIGHT

II — YOUR LIGHT IS ALWAYS ON

III — YOU ONLY HAVE TO SEE WHAT'S RIGHT IN FRONT OF YOU

IV — THERE'S A LARGER LIGHT GUIDING YOU

The first is the easiest to understand: You are light. First and foremost, conscious leadership is about shining and sharing your unique light for yourself and those you lead. At the most basic level, leaders recognize that everyone, including themselves, has a light within them that is unique, bright, purposeful.

Every human being has a light. Some call this the soul or spirit. Others might call it innate talent or the inner spark. Whatever you name it to be, your light has a unique quality to it—as unique as your thumbprint. Your light is the life force that brings vitality, purpose, wisdom, and direction to your path. It is your truest essence. Do you have a relationship with it? Do you look outside of yourself for answers first? Or do you turn within to listen to your light's unique wisdom, made especially for you?

Take a moment to look for your light as you read these words. Take your attention off these pages, close your eyes for just a moment, and direct your awareness inward. Notice your breath. Notice its rhythm. Who is the one breathing? Look behind your breath and feel your essence beyond your bones, muscles, organs, and physical form. Who is the one feeling?

Can you feel your light?

- What does it feel like?

- Does it have a color?

- Does it have a sensation?

- Does it have a boundary?

Leaders also light the way for others. Great leadership isn't having the most impressive role or title. Great leadership is the willingness to shine a light for others, especially when times are dark or unclear.

When things are clear and bright, people usually do well on their own. But when things become unclear, people need help. Leadership is about lighting the way for others in times of darkness, uncertainty, and difficulty—and often, about getting out of the way in times of abundance and success to allow others room to shine. It's about modeling what's possible and showing, rather than telling, the way forward.

If a leader is a light guiding the way for others, a leader must also have a light within them. A conscious leader turns within to look for their own light when they experience times of uncertainty and confusion.

Your Light Is Unique

As you work to become an increasingly conscious leader, you may find, as we have, that great leadership isn't about copying what someone else does—it's about finding your own unique way and helping others do the same.

Your light—your presence—is unique to you. Others can feel your light when you walk into the room. They can feel your absence when you leave. You have an energetic blueprint—a field that emanates from within you that goes with you wherever you go. Your light is beyond your physical form, and it can be the beacon that shines the way for you and others. It leaves an indelible impression on everything you interact with. How we shine it and where we shine it is up to us to choose.

To do so, you must become aware of who you are. As a conscious leader, you can always choose to become more awake and aware of your own light, noticing the quality of its presence— noticing when your light feels strong and vibrant, when it feels dim, what environments support its illumination, and which ones don't. When you become more aware of your own light, you can more intentionally choose where and how to show it and shine it.

You Are More than Body and Mind

JEN'S STORY:

From when I was a very young age, my mom would say, "The moment you take the field or walk into a room, Jennifer, everyone notices. You've got a powerful light." I never fully grasped what she meant.

Over the years, I felt the impact of my presence as a college athlete and into my business career. Strangers, teammates, and bosses would remark on my presence at some point or another. On some level, I resonated with what they were saying, but I still didn't really understand.

That was until I had the experience of leaving my body. I was twenty-one years old, fresh out of college, living in Salt Lake City, and training with a Jungian psychologist, healer, and spiritual teacher named Joyce. I lived on Joyce's property in a one-bedroom basement apartment nestled under the shadows of the Wasatch Mountains.

The ceilings were low, the light was dim, and the space was tiny, nudging me outside to connect with the organic garden that enveloped the property. Weeding the endless variety of vegetable and flower beds; harvesting pears, apples, grapes, and plums; and turning over the compost pile each week gave me the space and connection to nature my soul yearned for. It was also how I paid for my spiritual and metaphysical study.

One evening, I came home after playing in a lacrosse game with a torn ligament in my right knee. I decided to practice the healing work I was learning about. Unable to walk, I lay down on Joyce's couch.

She guided me into a deep meditative state, and I slipped into an altered state where my consciousness began to travel.

As if in a waking dream, I saw myself in a hospital room, lying on a stainless steel operating table. A surgeon and nurses hovered over me. After several minutes, I felt myself suddenly rise out of my body and float above the activity. Every nurse and doctor moved with a golden light—almost like a sunbeam—emanating out of their heart space. Some were consciously aware of their light, and some were not, but everyone had the glow.

In that moment, I had an overwhelming epiphany. "I am not my body, and I am not my mind. I am a soul," I realized. "This soul is my light. My light is on no matter what is happening with my body, and it's not only within me, but it is also within all of us!"

With this sudden awareness, I began being pulled toward a larger light—a tunnel that glowed with a soft white hue, as if I were inside an illuminated cloud. I could sense and see beings with soft luminescent shapes waiting for me on the other side, calling me to come. Then, I heard the most angelic melody, a profound collection of female voices singing in perfect harmony. They channeled wordless sounds through a symphony of octaves that felt heaven-sent.

An immense wave of unconditional love washed over me. It was strong yet soft, gentle yet powerful, warm yet palpable. This love-light filled every cell in my body, and I became infused with vibration and intense heat—like a wood-burning stove. In a state of pure bliss and suspended in time, I rested in silence, motionless for hours, until my light and awareness slowly returned to my body.

This was the shift that helped me realize I was something more than my body and mind. I am light. It's the root of the awareness I bring to my work with clients today to help them see and feel the same.

JEFF'S STORY:

Recently, I was at a family gathering—which in our family are always loud, happy, and somewhat chaotic affairs. The mood was even higher this time around, as the occasion was the birth of my niece Kayla's first baby, Olivia. Our extended family was thrilled to finally have a chance to meet this lovely girl, the first grandchild of my wife's parents and the start of a next generation for all of us.

I patiently waited my turn to hold this little bundle of joy. It had been almost three months since she was born, but schedules and daily life and the changes that come with having a newborn baby meant that this was the first time I had seen Kayla and her husband Joe since Olivia was born. And I had never met Olivia!

It was finally my turn. As I tried to revive my father-of-a-newborn muscles, I marveled at Olivia's awareness. At only a few months old, she was curious, observant, and in awe of everything around her. She watched me intently, then looked around the room. I could feel her light. I could see her totally in the moment. Then I looked around. A few of the adults were watching a football game. A few of the teenagers were on their phones.

It dawned on me: we don't need to try to be light. We are light! Being light is our natural state. When we come out of the womb, we are illuminated. We don't have to be taught how to shine.

Presence is our natural state, too. When we are born, we are completely and totally in the now. We actually learn how to become distracted. Getting back here, to right now, isn't a matter of learning any new skills. You already know them. You just need to take away all the other things pulling at your attention.

A leader is light. We all have it. Do you see yours?

The Connection Between Awareness and Presence

The awareness of your own light and the light of others is what we call presence.

Practicing presence is one of the greatest powers of a conscious leader. When we practice presence, we harness our ability to be conscious—a gift that most species are not privy to. It's a gift that has been bestowed on our human race, and it's our choice whether we make use of it or not.

The more we harness our innate ability to be aware of our presence—sensing the quality of our light and knowing the impression we make beyond our words and physical form—the more conscious we become. The more conscious we are, the more connected we feel.

Do you want to feel more connected? Of course you do. You are designed to be connected. We are all part of a communal species that has the privilege of being alive right now. Not all souls get the chance to have a physical body and the opportunity to live and learn in earth school at this time in history. For a lot of us here, it's all too easy to take that for granted.

That doesn't mean life is easy or pleasant. For many of us, it's not. But what if we didn't take this precious gift of being alive and conscious for granted—no matter our circumstances? Would we appreciate our experiences more? Would we be gentler with ourselves and others? Would we practice being here and now with more intention and attention? Would we be better leaders?

We believe so.

That said, we all have the choice to be conscious or not. Not everyone wants to be.

It can be easier to believe someone else's truth rather than your own. It can be easier to skim the surface than deeply listen to one's instincts and intuition.

When we rely on the outside world for our inner truth, we often fall into the trap of cultural conditioning. We unknowingly slip into a state of automatic actions, ancestral patterning, and unconscious reactions, dumbing ourselves down and subtly dismissing the intelligence of our own being.

But we have a choice to do things differently.

As a conscious leader, you recognize this choice point and feel the call to become more aware, turning within and using your presence for the greater good. You can sense that this is where your authentic power resides, and you are willing to courageously harness it.

Awareness Starts with Presence

Have you ever had the experience of seeing something new in a place you've lived in for a long time? Maybe it happened while you were driving home from work on a route you have driven ten times a week for the last five years. Or maybe you were driving your kids to school on a road you knew like the back of your hand.

Then suddenly, for some reason, your eye caught something you had never noticed before—a park nestled on the side of the road, a garden in front of someone's house, a funny sign you never knew was there. That's the power of being present.

Presence is the doorway into awareness—and deeper awareness unlocks the wonders of the world around us.

When you are present, you bring your attention to the moment at hand, here and now. Your increased attention leads you to notice more. And as you notice a greater range of inputs, you see, sense, and feel more expansively. As your capacity to perceive grows, you see patterns that you didn't used to notice. You become a master of connecting the dots.

When we talk to leaders who are becoming adept at practicing presence, they relate the feeling of experiencing the Divine at work firsthand. Events and circumstances that once appeared random become ordered in a mysterious way to offer them guidance. Signs and synchronicities seem to appear in their path for a reason.

As you become more adept at practicing presence, you become more curious about the cues and signs that appear on your path, which in turn leads you to learn, see, and sense more. As your ability to receive information increases, so does your attunement to the inner and outer forces at work.

Have you ever been in a conversation with someone and noticed that something else had captured their attention? Maybe you recognized that their body language didn't match the words they were using. Maybe they interrupted you or seemed to have a hard time focusing on the conversation.

In short, you can tell they aren't present.

On a coaching call, we noticed Amy, an executive director of a large nonprofit, come onto the video screen differently than normal. Her shoulders were drooped, her eyes looked sad, and she appeared physically depleted. Her words didn't have the clarity or energy they usually did. She spoke with long pauses, making it difficult to understand what she was trying to convey. She seemed lost for words.

It felt like we had to pull anything of substance out of her. This was not the Amy we had coached and counseled over the past two years.

Since her other team members were on the call, it didn't feel appropriate to address the dissonance publicly. We decided to end the call early and reach out to Amy privately. When we did, we shared what we had observed and asked if she was okay.

"Oh, wow," she said. "That's not exactly how I'm feeling, but yeah—something's off. I didn't realize I was giving such obvious signals." She confided in us that she felt overwhelmed and stuck, not knowing how to convince her boss that she and her team were experiencing major burnout.

Her ability to share that with us allowed us an opening to address the real issue at hand—burnout—which in turn led us to coach her on new and honest ways to communicate with her boss about what she needed.

Our experience with Amy is an example of how presence is connected to the practice of deep listening—hearing not only what is shared with you from the outside world, but also what is shared with you from the whispers of your own intuition and heart. Because we were present with Amy, we could notice things beyond the words she used.

Deep, present listening allows you to hear not only the words someone uses to communicate, but also where they are coming from *as* they communicate. Your presence picks up on the overt and subtle cues of expression, inviting you into a new level of multidimensional awareness. With practice, you can accelerate the art of perception and come to understand that life is less linear than you might have been led to believe. Before you know it, you become adept at seeing the current that gives life energy and meaning as you experience the interconnection of everything for yourself.

You stop looking outside for answers and become the leader you're looking for.

It's an amazing feeling.

We've found that the more we practice bringing our full presence to the present moment, the more available we can be to the muse—the creative intelligence that makes up everything. We become better equipped to respond freshly, uniquely, and authentically to what shows up, and make ourselves available for what wants to come through us (which is perfectly tailored to the need in the moment).

However, it is so much easier said than done. Whether it is texts that flash on our computer screens, children coming into the room while we are on a Zoom call, or endless phone notifications that draw our attention away from what we are doing, the interruptions seem constant.

On some occasions, the distractions get so ridiculously comical that in order to get some peace and quiet, we must leave the house or office. Other days, the external distractions seem to be minimal, but the internal distractions of worry and stress take over.

Simply put, bringing awareness to the times when you are not present is as powerful a tool as noticing when you are.

Aligning with Your Light

Once you become aware of your own light, you have a choice whether to align with it or not. As you bring your awareness to the present moment, you can start to pay attention to the inner and outer clues that can help you choose that alignment.

The clues are always around. Have you ever felt a pit in your stomach or a flutter in your heart? Of course—every human has. Our body is one of the clearest channels of intelligence. It knows what we need and when we need it. It is always speaking to you. Are you always listening?

When you walk into a room, how does your body feel? Does it want to lean in or out? When you are in a conversation with someone, do you expand or contract? Do you find yourself absorbed in the conversation, or do you find yourself searching for something to say? Do you find yourself at rapt attention, or do you notice that you are squirming in your chair? Often, you will find that when you bring your focus to your body during an experience, interaction, or conversation, you will hear your body's whispers. Instead of brushing them off or overlooking those cues, you can choose to notice more deeply how the innate intelligence of your physical form works for you.

When we talk about things we care about, our body responds. How does your body speak to you?

JEN'S STORY:

When I am speaking my truth and engaged in work I am passionate about, I light up. My eyes get bigger and more focused. My voice gets louder, and I articulate my words with a clearer enunciation and distinction. My neck flushes as blood flow naturally speeds up to match my increased heart rate.

This uncontrollable trait used to embarrass the hell out of me. When keynoting or public speaking, I'd find myself planning my outfit to include a scarf that I'd conveniently use to cover up my neck so I wouldn't give the audience the impression I was nervous. Later, I learned and appreciated that this was my body's signal, showing me what I deeply cared about. I slowly began to drop the scarf and talk openly on stage about my natural performance response as a teaching tool for how the body automatically responds when we are expressing our passions.

JEFF'S STORY:

One of my earliest memories is sitting at my grandparents' dinner table at their house on the farm. The table would be replete with simply prepared but excellent food, most of it grown on the property. Deep green beans, steaming mashed potatoes, and glazed ham decorated the plain tablecloth.

My grandfather would start grace—but he almost never finished it, because every time, without fail, he would break down in tears. Overwhelmed by the combination of unbearable sadness and unspeakable gratitude that comes from eighty years on the planet, he could never get all the words out.

That's one way my inner light aligns with my emotions and physical body, often without me even knowing it is coming—I'll find myself tearing up. It's sometimes a tad embarrassing, because I've found a way to cry about everything from Star Wars and playing piano to customer analytics and clever strategic positioning. But I've learned to recognize it as a sign that I care. Rarely are the tears linked to sadness in any way—they are linked to some reservoir of deep emotion, often elation, connection, community, inspiration, and most often, the simple awe of being connected to the spirit of creation.

I'm so grateful to my grandfather for showing me that emotions are meant to be expressed, not hidden away.

How does your body speak to you? Can you tell when you are aligned or misaligned with your light? When you talk about something you care about, what happens? When you don't want to do something, do you cross your arms and move away? Or like us, do anything but the task at hand?

How the Body Speaks

Our body is one of our greatest alignment tools. It shows us when we are aligned with our light and when we are not before we intellectually know it. When our body speaks to us, whether it be through exhilaration, elation, and energy, or through pain, discomfort, or a sensation of dis-ease, we are called to listen. It's all too easy to brush it off as a reaction to something external, whether that be the situation, food, environment, or stress. But what if it's a sign to help us change our course? What if it is telling us when we are aligned to our light and when we are not?

Attunement to the body is one of the core tools we practice in our executive coaching and retreats to help conscious leaders like you align to their light. It is simple—and incredibly effective.

What Lights You Up?

Take a moment to settle into your body as you read these words. Notice your breath, this incredible gift you were given today that helps you feed and express your light. Give thanks for it, as many souls were not given this blessing today.

Allow your attention to drop from your head space to your heart space. Imagine a gentle, soft, glowing sun rising in the center of your chest. You can see its rays illuminating your physical form from the inside out. Your cells, muscles, organs, and bones begin to shimmer and glow. You expand as the light becomes brighter and larger in and around you. You sense your light field, your presence, and your essence. It is infinite, and it wants all aspects of your personality and expression to align with it.

In this state of expansion, you ask yourself, "What lights me up?" You allow the answers to bubble up into your awareness. Memories, scenes, adventures, hobbies, and explorations float into your consciousness. You feel delight. You feel light. Allow symbols, faces, and any scenes to become known to you. Allow the light that you are to infuse energy and vitality into what brings you joy.

Then, when you are ready, bring your attention back to your breath, noticing its natural intelligence of knowing when to inhale and exhale without you having to control it. Bring your attention back to these words. Take a moment to pause and write down what occurred to you.

What lights you up?

Making It Simple: The Trinity of Alignment

All too often, we make life, success, and performance more complicated than they need to be. We condition ourselves to believe that we must do more to be more. But what if that wasn't true at all? What if *being* was the key to unlocking the life we wish to have? What if we were meant to be lit up? What if joy really was our birthright? We believe that it is.

At Plenty, we use a tool called the Trinity of Alignment. It is a simple way to help conscious leaders bring clarity, focus, and performance to themselves and the people they lead. It's a tool to connect our passions, our strengths, and the business need at hand. You can imagine it as a triangle, where your passions lie on one side of the base, your strengths lie on the other side of the base, and the need sits at the top of the pyramid (of the business, project, family, community, and so forth).

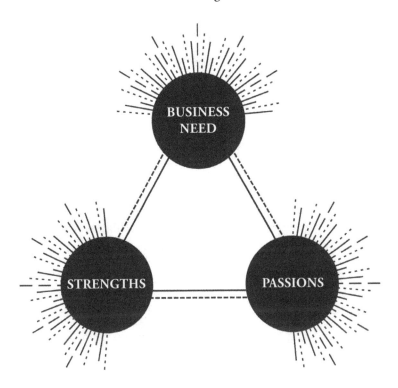

When we align what we naturally care about, what we are great at, and the need at hand, we create synergy and connection. The result is performance, efficiency, joy, fulfillment, and realized potential. Our lives light up.

What lights each of us up may differ. That's perfectly okay. In fact, that is exactly how we've been designed. What lights you up can't be forced or manufactured—you either care about something or you don't. You're either energized by a subject, cause, or conversation or you're not.

The same goes for strengths. You have strengths that are uniquely yours. Your skills may have developed over your life, or you may have simply been born with them. Our bet is that your strengths directly correlate to the things you care about. Instead of trying to turn your weaknesses into strengths, what if you simply amplified and channeled what you are great at toward the things that light you up?

When you align your passions and strengths with the need at hand, you generate energy from the inside. Think of it as intrinsic motivation that results from aligning what you care about with what you are great at. You don't have to wait for someone else to tell you what to do—and more importantly, you don't have to tell your team what to do either! Natural internal motivation gets harnessed when these elements are defined and aligned, and efficiency and productivity result.

Finding Flow

We can also find alignment by noticing the current. Where is the flow of the river taking us? Where is there momentum in our day? Noticing these cues can help us shed the outdated cultural conditioning that tells us our worth is intertwined with the effort we put out. That's just not true. What would your life be like if you could let the river take you closer and closer to your light without having to paddle upstream? It would likely be a hell of a lot easier and a lot more enjoyable.

Again, that's not to say that you don't have to invest your time, energy, and self in your goals. Practice, repetitions, habits, and hard work are prerequisites for success. But think of it this way:

if you love cycling and hate running, would you rather do a 10K footrace or a century bike ride? If you love public speaking and hate accounting, would you rather do a sales presentation or a budget?

What we're pointing to is that while work is usually required, effort is optional. When you're doing something you love, the work actually feels effortless. It is fun.

Have you ever found yourself immersed in a project that has captured your imagination, only to look up and realize that hours have passed? That flow state is a sign of alignment. This is what aligning to our light feels like. It's easier. It's freer. It requires a lot less doing and a lot more being. It's an invitation to harness the authentic nature of our existence while releasing the self-induced pressure to become something other than we are.

Leading with Intention

Once we become more aware of what lights us up (and what doesn't), and where we are aligned and where we are not, we can harness the power of intention.

In the spring of 2020, no one could have predicted what was about to unfold: Lockdowns, social distancing, school closings, flight groundings, mask mandates, and new norms suddenly emerged. It's likely none of these experiences were on anyone's strategic plan. In fact, our clients' strategic plans were completely upended. We experienced the opposite with our clients. Many businesses closed. Budgets that were once predicted to be steady and stable got blown up with the COVID-19 pandemic.

This is the limitation of goals—they work best in predictable, controllable environments. But we aren't living in that type of environment anymore. And importantly, goals set a target for what you want to achieve—but most of life is spent in the process of working toward that achievement, not in the achievement itself. If 95 percent of your time is spent on the path rather than the destination, doesn't it make sense to spend some time reflecting on what you want the journey to be like?

This is where intention comes in. Intention is a powerful tool conscious leaders use to set the tone for how they want to feel during the journey of an experience. Conscious leaders recognize that they have the power to create the experience they want to have, and as such, they command their attention to bring it forth. Setting intention is a concrete way for conscious leaders to call forth the energy and feelings they wish to experience.

Intention works because it channels our attention. And whatever we bring our attention to, we bring our energy to. Said another way, wherever we focus, we form. Or, whatever we feed, we grow.

Conscious leaders set intentions to point their team members toward what is desired. Those intentions also invite the team to help actualize the desired goal. For instance, if you give a group of bright minds at a for-profit product company the intention to collaborate on becoming more sustainable in their operations, they will come up with brilliant ideas that are both inspiring and actionable. This happens because every group member has been invited to bring forth their unique ideas and passions toward a shared intent. The more diverse the group, the richer the outcome.

Conscious leaders align with the light within, set intentions that align to that light, and invite others in to share in the intention.

At Plenty, we use the power of intention for every client call, team meeting, retreat, or engagement we lead, and we are always in awe of what transpires when we do. We've found that setting an intention at the beginning of our day, at the start of a business meeting, to kick off a week, or to launch a new year gives power to our goals and desires. Often, when we set an intention, we experience the desire we invited in. When this happens, we get to witness our power in action.

For example, intention has become a powerful part of our sales process. We set our intention to create a mutually beneficial outcome for both our client and ourselves. We approach the sales meeting as an opportunity to serve, not sell. We communicate our intention by asking, "How can we best use your time?" We know that if we approach from that intention, we'll create value for the client right away.

How can you harness the power of your intention?

Awareness, Alignment, and Intention with Your Light

Being a conscious leader means playing with an interconnected set of practices:

- Closing the congruency gap between how you view yourself and how others experience you.

- Being intentional about how you want to feel at the end of the day, at the end of a meeting, during a conversation, or after a project has been completed.

- Channeling that intention in a way that allows others to create it with you.

- Being mindful about your time and where you place your attention, understanding that both are a precious gift.

- Getting clear on when to say "Yes" and when to say "No," because you are present enough to know which answer aligns best with your light.

- Becoming aware of the roles you play—consciously and unconsciously—and working to align your roles with what brings out the best in you, so you can help others do the same.

Written this way, actively practicing awareness, alignment, and intention can sound like a lot of work!

But we're pointing to the opposite. It's not about doing more. It is about stripping layers away so you can be fully attuned to your deepest values. It's wiping the dust off the window so the full, bright light can shine through. Decisions become quicker because you know what works for you and what doesn't. Your professional life becomes more fulfilling because you are increasingly centered on what you like and what you don't, so you learn to delegate or decline work that isn't a good fit.

Where you choose to direct your light makes all the difference in the experience you weave. With greater awareness and a commitment to better alignment, you can intentionally choose where you show up, where you don't, and how you do so. You can bring your light with you wherever you are, to whomever you meet.

But what about when you're feeling confused, or tired, or discouraged? What about the times you can't even see your own light, let alone share it with anyone else?

We'll consider those situations next.

PRACTICE POINTS

PRACTICING THE FIRST LIGHT

You Are Light

Listen to Your Body

There's no better tool for awareness and alignment than the practice of listening to your own body. All too often, we are stuck in our heads, listening to our thoughts, using reason, and intellectualizing our choices—and so we forget to listen to the cues and signals our body is sending us on an ongoing basis. Vague unease in the stomach, tense shoulder muscles, a twitch in the cheek that happens before a particular meeting each week—these are all messages, too. As you learn to direct your attention to your whole body, you can tap into the intelligence that is within you, always sending you the information you need to attune to your own wellbeing.

Here are a few questions that you can practice asking yourself to help you become more aware of what's working and what's not.

1. What signals is my body sending me in this moment?

2. In this moment, does my heart feel open and safe? Or closed and protected?

3. Is my breath shallow or deep? Am I holding it in?

4. In this moment, do I feel energized or depleted?

We're not suggesting you abandon logic. We're pointing to the idea that logic is only one of many methods you have for noticing and working through an issue. If you only spend time in your head, you can miss most of the information you're receiving and sending.

Become the Auditor

Pretend you are an auditor, and you've been hired to assess the current state of your life and help you see what is really there. As someone with a neutral stance, you're not attached to what you see. You don't have a story or a history—rather, you have mastered the unfiltered eye of the observer with a lot of detachment.

Notice what you notice:

- Do you want to move closer to them or further away?

- Do you find yourself distracted and tuning out?

- Do you find yourself enthralled by what is being shared, wanting more?

Use the Trinity of Alignment

Whether you are leading your family, your children, your business, or your team, knowing where to lean in and where to lean out can help harness your gifts with greater ease and fulfillment.

Understanding what you're passionate about (what you care about) and what you are great at (your strengths) can help you align with the need at hand.

1. **Inventory your passions**. List all the things, activities, places, subjects, and ideas that bring you joy. Add causes, subjects, topics, and states of being that you're curious about and interested in.

2. **Inventory your strengths**. Make a list of all the skills you have. What are you great at? What comes easily to you? What are you naturally good at? Where are you most comfortable?

3. **Inventory the need**. What does your business need to grow in revenue, impact, and fulfillment? What does your family need to live a healthy and happy life? What does your community need to connect and grow? What does your team need to align and perform?

4. **Now look at the three lists**. Are there places that the three inventories intersect—areas that you enjoy, that you do well at, and that are needed? Those are places to spend your time. On the other hand, needs that don't align with your passions or strengths are crying out for delegation or outside assistance. And passions or strengths that don't fill an immediate need are invitations to grow and expand your reach—because surely someone can use the fruits of the passions you love to pursue.

Flesh Out Your Fear

In a similar fashion as the practice point above, make a different kind of list—a list of fears. Write down your biggest worries, your concerns, and the fears that have been with you since you were little—or the fears that have most recently found you.

Once you have your list, remind yourself of the powerful acronym that author Neale Donald Walsch coined for FEAR, "False Evidence Appearing Real." Investigate your fears.

- Have your fears come to fruition?

- What would be the worst thing that would happen if they did?

- Are they your fears, or were they seeded by someone or something else?

- Are they coming from the news or a past experience?

Flesh out your fears and allow yourself to see them for what they are. Allow this awareness to bring you back here, to the present moment. In various forms, this practice has been championed since the times of Buddhist and Stoic philosophers to build both resilience and acceptance.

Notice Your Excitement

If everything is energy, then energy itself helps inform what step to take next. Observing when and why we get excited may seem all too simple—so very simple that we find ourselves automatically overriding and ignoring this information if we're not careful. Instead of writing your excitement off, what would happen if you paid more attention to its wisdom?

Grab your journal or a piece a paper and answer these questions:

- When do I feel most alive?

- What subjects or ideas make me smile?

- Where do I feel drawn?

- What am I curious about?

- Where am I procrastinating or avoiding things?

- Where do I feel drained?

These are all clues and cues to the light inside you that can guide your way.

Ask Your Light

Grab a pen and paper, or sit at your computer and open your favorite digital journal application. We love using Evernote or Day One for our online keepsakes. Set the energy for your space by either lighting a candle, putting on your favorite peaceful music, or listening to a guided meditation (check out www.plentyconsulting.com/meditations if you don't have one you like already) to help yourself quiet and center.

Begin by asking your light what you need to know now. You may have a specific question that comes to mind that you want an answer to. Or you may want to explore the force that is pulling you in another direction. Pretend that your inner light has all the answers and is waiting for you to ask so it can share! Then ask and listen. Free write whatever comes to mind until you feel a sense of completion.

When you are done, take a break, and then come back and read what your light wants you to know.

Notice what your light has written. What wisdom does it have for you?

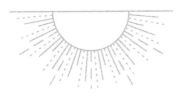

CHAPTER 5

The Second Light
Your Light Is Always On

When we talk with leaders about the First Light of Conscious Leadership, You Are Light, we often hear people acknowledge that *sometimes* they can see how they bring their full light to themselves and others. They will say things like, "Yes, when I'm at my best, I can see how I make the world brighter for my team."

Then just as quickly, they'll say, "But sometimes I don't feel that way at all." They'll talk about how sometimes they can be rash, egotistical, nervous, or anxious. They'll talk with regret about moments when they didn't conduct themselves the way they wanted to. "But what if," we ask them, "your light is always on, no matter how you feel?"

Imagine you are standing on the beach, looking at the waves cutting through the ocean on a warm, windy summer day. Large, white, puffy clouds fill the deep blue sky as you listen to the crash of water on the sand.

The sun feels warm to your skin, but every few minutes you get chilled as a cloud moves in front of the sun. Though it is warm out, you find yourself pulling a sweatshirt on and off with the movement of the clouds.

Can you feel it?

Now consider: When the clouds cover the sun, has the sun vanished? Is the sky less blue behind the clouds?

Of course not. You realize the sun hasn't vanished—it is only hidden from view for a bit. In fact, as you look across the beach, you can probably see places where the sun is still shining.

In the same way, what if in your darkest moments, you could still count on your light to shine the way?

You see, it doesn't matter if you are in a happy mood or a low mood. Like the sun behind the clouds, your light is always shining. It keeps shining whether you feel connected or lonely, empowered or encumbered. Your light emanates your true essence regardless of your feelings. Whether you perceive it or not, your light comes with you wherever you go.

Often, we see that the leaders we work with view their strengths as they might view abilities in a video game—traits they can use occasionally, that then require time to cool down and recharge. But do those abilities ever disappear? If you are having a wonderful day, and then get a phone call from a client who criticizes you, has your light diminished in any way?

What if your light could never be diminished?

Even in your least confident moments, you still have access to all the confidence you've ever learned in life. In your most egotistical moments, you have access to all your humility. In your most self-deprecating moments, you are still connected to all your inner strength. In your deepest times of doubt and uncertainty, you still have the light of trust and faith.

The quality of your light doesn't change. Your feelings might change; your thoughts about yourself might change. Yet, like a dirty windshield changes the view but not the road, your sad feelings or insecure thoughts haven't changed who you are.

The two of us have noticed that the more fully we explore and experience this concept, the more we move through the highs and lows of being human with ease and grace. We loosen our grip on our feelings and trust in the flow of our ever-changing moods. When we do so, we drop the need to be anything other than what we are.

To be honest, this has not always been comfortable. But, with practice, it has gotten a lot easier. After years of trying to be the "best leaders we can be," to hold ourselves to high standards and uncompromising ideals, we needed to learn how to give ourselves permission to be human. That's the first step.

Being Aware of Being Human

From a young age, we both have been natural leaders. We've been idealists, dreamers, and visionaries wired to help create a better world. How we articulated and expressed that drive was individually different, but it was certainly the connecting thread that first united our lights over twenty-five years ago.

Like most idealistic leaders, our leadership was often cloaked in an unconscious drive to please, prove, and strive to be the best.

This inner drive would fuel our self-confidence, most noticeably when we felt accomplished and seen.

Yet, when things unraveled, as often happens to big dreamers, our self-confidence would unravel, too. Accepting our human-ness was hard. We had set the bar so high for ourselves that when things didn't perfectly go our way, it was uncomfortable to accept our own limitations. Does that sound familiar?

JEN'S STORY:

The year was 2015, and I was visiting the office of Scott Kelly, a dear friend and fellow performance coach. At the time, my company was called Healthy Happy Human BEings—a membership-based education and networking platform.

I was sitting in a cozy chair surrounded by four other people. A warm fireplace that crackled and popped. We were all participating in a weekend retreat on the Three Principles, studying mind, consciousness, and thought. As I sat there listening to Scott share his knowledge, my attention began to float around the room. I remember daydreaming a bit as my thoughts began to loosen and lighten. I felt relaxed and peaceful after days of learning, connecting, and being.

Suddenly, my attention meandered toward the back of the closed office door, and I began to stare at the poster that adorned it. The poster marketed an upcoming Healthy Happy Human BEings event in Park City. As I focused on the poster, the word "Human" suddenly jumped out at me. It was as if I had never seen that word before.

And, then it hit me. This poster was my poster! This company was my company! Up until this point, I realized that everything I spoke about, wrote about, and convened about was centered around being "Healthy and Happy." I would use "Healthy and Happy" as shorthand for the marketing materials and events I would produce.

I remember saying out loud, "Oh my God, I've never really seen or used the word Human in my own company name!"

I realized in that split second of awareness that I had never fully given myself permission to be human before, either. It was difficult for me to be messy. In that moment, I saw the pressure I always placed on myself: to keep my hair looking good, my outfits a certain style, my communications well formulated, and my command of a room pitch-perfect through all of my professional ladder climbing. I recognized how I'd worked to be top-tier in my athletic pursuits and was ceaselessly vigilant about saying and doing the "right" things in relationships. Racing away from my humanness had characterized my whole life.

I had required myself to be healthy and happy (and to help others be the same), all the while missing out on the gift of allowing myself to be human. It may sound ridiculous, and it certainly sounds ridiculous to me as I write this. But it was real for me. As soon as I realized this, I dropped into a deeper vulnerability. I began to loosen my grip, and the unconscious tensions that held me subtly melted away. Over time, I began to feel more peaceful, steady, and okay with the ups and downs of life. I began feeling okay when I didn't feel okay.

JEFF'S STORY:

It was spring 2011—eighteen months after my dad was killed, and six months after I had started to put myself back together. I had been re-engaging in work, encouraged by patient business partners, a great team, and supportive clients.

Things were coming together for me personally, but as we approached the summer, our executive team of eight or nine senior leaders was feeling a bit stuck. The company's growth had flattened, and it felt like we had issues with communication and performance that we weren't truly resolving.

We decided to hold a two-day retreat, and hired a professional facilitator to help lead the conversation.

As I met with her to plan the sessions, she asked, "Are you open to using a leadership styles survey?" She suggested Myers-Briggs, probably the most famous of all the styles indexes, as a way to help us all get to know one another better.

When it came time for the retreat, I'll never forget the feeling as the facilitator handed out the Myers-Briggs results to each one of us. After briefly reviewing each person's results, she turned to me and said, "Here's the feedback the team wants to give you."

I was caught off-guard. "Um. What?"

I looked around the room. Some of my team members were looking down at their laps. Others looked as surprised as

I was. The room had gone completely quiet. I could hear a lawnmower outside in the hotel garden.

"From the interviews I conducted with your team, there are some things everyone needs you to do differently," the facilitator began. "You like to dive bomb into issues—you stay too uninvolved most of the time, then jump unexpectedly into micromanagement. When you speak, you have to listen, too—you tend to take all the air out of the room. And, you aren't very good at empowerment or delegation, and so you underutilize the skill in the room."

And so on! It continued for more than a few minutes. With the benefit of hindsight, I can see the merit in all the comments I received. The feedback was direct, spot-on, and helpful. But at the time, I felt blindsided—and hurt.

I'd love to say I took the feedback well, but I didn't. I did my best to listen, but I became aloof and defensive, a reaction that got even worse as we left the meeting to do a team-building exercise at a local go-kart track. I couldn't get my car started, got rammed by my team members more than a few times, and ended the race dead last.

It felt like a fitting metaphor for the day!

Mike—one of my business partners, mentors, and most of all friends—came up to me at the bar afterward. He smiled at me. "Do you want a beer, or do you need to move directly to something stronger?"

I winced. "Ouch. Is it that obvious?"

Mike laughed. "Well, that was probably more focused on you than we intended it to be! But I'll tell you what you always tell us: the feedback is a gift. Take what is useful and forget the rest. But doesn't it say something about how much this team respects you that they care enough to tell you what they need?"

He instantly lightened me up. Jeez. I didn't have to be perfect; more importantly, I wasn't. My need to be great was keeping me from getting better. If I could step beyond that, I'd find the joy that comes from receiving—and acting on—feedback.

Being aware of our humanness—giving ourselves a break—is an important practice of leading ourselves and others. If we can't give ourselves permission to be messy, have good days and bad ones, succeed and fail, disappoint people, say the wrong thing, and rise and fall, then what message are we modeling for others? After all, conscious leaders model the way.

But it's about more than "allowing ourselves to be human," which kind of sounds like "it's okay to make mistakes." We're pointing to something deeper than that. What we're trying to convey is not only that our humanness is an explanation for our mistakes. *Our mistakes are the foundational signature of our humanness.*

We don't need to eliminate our mistakes or protect ourselves from them. Should we learn from them? Absolutely. *Our mistakes become the core of the lessons that lead us to growth.* People who don't allow themselves the messiness of being human may have safe existences, but they also end up having dull lives. The goal of life isn't to be infallible. The goal of life is to live fully. We were designed to do so.

The Nature of Thought

Have you ever gone to bed feeling great only to wake up the next morning not wanting to get up? Have you ever felt hopeful and excited in one moment, only to have that blissful state instantly shift thanks to sudden news that overwhelms you with fear? Of course you have, and we have too. That's the nature of being human—it's an up-and-down journey of highs and lows, ebbs and flows.

We both have learned a great deal from a philosophy called the Three Principles, a way of viewing the connectedness between thoughts and feelings that we mentioned a few pages earlier. The principles were first articulated by a philosopher and author named Sydney Banks. He was searching for a way to explain his own anxiety, and a friend said to him, essentially, "You aren't insecure—you only think you are."

For most of us, this retort would have been patently unhelpful, but for Banks, it was a revelation. A core idea of the Three Principles is that our changing emotions come from our changing thoughts. Our thoughts change in ways we're not even aware of as our brain process millions of pieces of stimuli and information from our stomachs, our hearts, our skin, our eyes, our ears, our environment, and so forth. That's why one of the keys to conscious leadership is awareness.

Perhaps you have reflected on a disagreement with a family member or coworker and found yourself getting riled up all over again. Or maybe you've found yourself looking back on the death of a family member and ended up in tears.

What changed? The world around you didn't change. What changed was your own thoughts, and those thoughts then created feelings. We often work with leaders who, when sharing a moment of achievement, find themselves full of pride as they tell it. And in the same way, when sharing a moment of conflict, find themselves frustrated and angry.

The way we are designed as physical beings, we take in stimuli throughout our body, then send messages about it to the brain, and the brain sends out thoughts as a result. The thoughts tell us if we should be excited or scared, nervous or joyful. You can try this yourself: Imagine you are eating a lemon or a sour candy. You can quickly make your mouth water and pucker up, experiencing a feeling of sourness, by simply invoking that thought. It's the same as reliving an argument and finding yourself angry all over again. It's amazing when you realize it.

In his incredible book *Inside-Out Revolution: The Only Thing You Need to Know to Change Your Life Forever*, author and coach Michael Neill relates learning this idea from mystic and philosopher Syd Banks. He describes the concept simply as, "We're living in the feeling of our thinking."[4] In other words, what we *think* determines how we feel. We literally digest our thinking. It's a groundbreaking way to view mental health and mindfulness in general, and you can find elements of the Three Principles in modern mindfulness, wellbeing, and therapy.

---

4 Michael Neill, *The Inside-Out Revolution: The Only Thing You Need to Know to Change Your Life Forever* (Carlsbad: Hay House, 2013).

Understanding that your thoughts create your feelings and not the reverse is a massive game-changer. It's the difference between riding down the river's rapids gritting your teeth and swearing versus laughing with glee. You enter the current of the river and the ride becomes easier, more fun, and way more enjoyable.

Have you ever noticed that when you are in a bad mood, everything seems to go wrong? You wake up irritated, spill the coffee, bump into a door, and drop your glasses on the way to the car. The traffic is endless and when you get to the office, you feel like you have a huge pile of thankless work to do.

Conversely, when your thoughts are positive, things seem to flow. You feel present and unhurried when you wake up. The coffee you make tastes fantastic. As you drive your car down the road, you hit every green light and appreciate the synchronicity. When you get to the office, you already feel productive, organized, and on top of your day.

By becoming more aware of the role our thinking plays in shaping our experience, we can learn to use our minds more effectively and create a more positive and fulfilling life. Often, that doesn't mean talking ourselves out of low feelings—instead, we learn to simply notice them and let them pass without attachment, like the clouds at the beach on a sunny summer day. Understanding the connection between thinking and feeling helps us become more aware, aligned, and intentional throughout our days.

It's a practice—there's a discipline involved in not immediately digesting every thought your brain is trying to feed you. But there's a huge amount of freedom and empowerment that comes from that discipline.

As Michael Neil writes, "When our thoughts look real, we live in a world of suffering. When they look subjective, we live in a world of choice. When they look arbitrary, we live in a world of possibility. And when we see them as illusory, we wake up inside a world of dreams."[5]

JEFF'S STORY:

My youngest son Danny has started to fall in love with golf. Like everyone in the family, he tends to go all-in on the things he enjoys, which means he is golfing nearly every chance he can—sometimes well over thirty-six holes a day.

Danny doesn't drive yet, so his new love of the sport means that I'm golfing a lot more, too. Make no mistake—I'm pretty bad, and he often beats me. But I've enjoyed spending time with him. I marvel at how time changes things—ten years ago, golf was an unneeded distraction away from my family. Now, it has become a way to bond with them.

A few weeks ago, we were waiting to tee off on a particularly cloudy day. The weather hadn't looked promising, so we almost didn't go, but at the last minute we decided to chance it. Which left us sitting at the first hole, where we shivered in our windbreakers as storm clouds rolled in.

Just as the group in front of us hit their opening drives, the rain started. We watched as the people scattered about, complaining loudly about the weather. One commented

5 Michael Neill, *The Inside-Out Revolution: The Only Thing You Need to Know to Change Your Life Forever* (Carlsbad: Hay House, 2013).

about how much better it had been yesterday. Another remarked that it was supposed to clear up later, and maybe they should come back tomorrow? A third fiddled with an umbrella, as the fourth rummaged through a golf bag for a coat.

I was struck at the microcosm of perspectives happening in front of me. Regret for the past, a lament for the future, the temptation to avoid, and the need to control all played out in something as simple as four adults coping with a spring rainstorm.

I looked at Danny. "Well, champ, what do you think?"

Danny shrugged. With the wisdom of ages, he said, "I guess we're going to get wet."

The power of thought!

The Power of Perspective

There's real power in this perspective, as we take up the invitation to *be* the reality we wish to see. A lot of our work involves helping leaders say yes to this invitation by seeing facts as they are, without attaching feelings to them. It's amazing, though, how often the feelings take the lead. Even the most "logical" people we work with are often taking their thoughts at face value without stepping back from them.

Several years ago, we worked with the executive team of an international nonprofit. They called us to do strategic planning, curiously, because they needed help ramping the organization down. Their fundraising had been declining, and they had decided to cease operations. They wanted to create a plan to do it in an orderly way.

As part of the discovery, we reviewed their financials. We were amazed to see the amount of cash they had on their balance sheet. In fact, it was the equivalent of about eighteen months of income for the organization. We'd worked with organizations twenty times their size who didn't carry that much cash.

At the retreat, we asked the team about it. "We hate to break it to you," we said. "But you don't look like an organization that needs to go out of business."

The team was silent for a moment. Finally, the CFO said, "Well, if we don't raise any more money, we will go out of business." It took all the restraint we had not to shout, *"Yeah—in a year and a half!"*

We politely suggested that instead of using that time to close, what if they used that time to grow a new funding channel? It required some facilitation, but eventually everyone agreed that there were two ways of looking at the fact of having eighteen months of cash on hand. One thought was, "This will eventually disappear." The other thought was, "This will fund our growth." The reality was the same—the thought is what changed.

It was rewarding to get a call from the CEO a year later that they had received a five-year grant worth $25 million to broaden the scope of their work as a result of the strategic plan we created together.

Staying Aligned When Everything Is Dark

So, how can you loosen the tie between your identity and your feelings? The answer lies, once again, in becoming more aware that you are thinking and being gentle with your naturally changing moods. You are not your thoughts. Despite how you feel, your light is always on. It comes with you wherever you go.

How do you stay aligned to your inner light when you feel like you are having a really bad day? Trust that your unique, intelligent light is always on no matter how you feel.

JEN'S STORY:

I was lying on the bed in my hotel room, fully dressed and made up, sobbing. It was 2016, and Jeff and I had recently joined forces. We were about to meet to head over to a large event we were keynoting for one of our large nonprofit clients, an organization whose mission was to help find the cure to end breast cancer.

I was suddenly overcome with thoughts of not being good enough, not being prepared enough, and unconsciously believing I had nothing to say that would be meaningful. Caught up in these thinking patterns, I became paralyzed with stage fright. The more I attached to my insecure thoughts, the more they looped, and the more I felt alone, scared, and downright awful. I didn't want to let our client, Jeff, or myself down.

At the time, I had no idea nor understanding of where these feelings were coming from. I had keynoted, facilitated, and spoken to large audiences hundreds of times before in my career. I had performed in so many situations like this—in the business world and on the athletic field. I had studied and received my degree in psychology and sports performance, so I knew what happens when our bodies and minds prepare to perform. But none of that mattered—nor did it even cross my mind—as anxiety pinned me to the bed.

I tried to rehearse and search for anything of relevance and came up short every time. I was spinning and I was lost. I just could not see any way that I had connection or authenticity when talking about breast cancer.

With Jeff's support and encouragement, I pulled myself together and did the best I could. The courage I had practiced for years kicked in and helped me rise to the occasion, although I certainly didn't feel at my best. Moving stories of loss, grief, survival, and deep care were shared throughout the day. Hearing them made me feel grateful and helped to soften my self-inflicted turmoil. Somehow, I got through.

Later that night, Jeff and I were debriefing and processing. During our exchange, he kindly reminded me of my mom's experience with . . . guess what? Breast cancer! Yup, exactly. My mom literally was five years into her remission that day. I was so caught up in my own thinking that I didn't even recall the rich, authentic, personal story I could have shared from my lived experience—a story filled with hope, encouragement, and inspiration.

This is what thought does. It takes over. It blinds us. It looks so believable, and if we aren't careful, we easily buy what we are selling ourselves—without question and certainly without discretion.

We can take the pressure off ourselves as we begin to witness that our feelings of discouragement, self-doubt, and fear are natural. Perhaps low feelings like these aren't designed to tell us we should quit, surrender, or run and hide. Perhaps these feelings are precisely designed to remind us of the innate courage, resolve, and confidence we have within ourselves—new feelings on the other side of a new thought.

If we take feelings of doubt and fear at face value, we always live small and afraid. If we see them for what they are—as indicators of the quality of our current thinking—we can ease up on ourselves, trusting that new feelings are only one thought away.

You Are the Mirror

The great news is that we don't have to go at this work alone. That's because we've been given the gift of being human. One of the amazing traits of human beings is that we are a communal species. We are not designed to be alone. We literally need each other to thrive.

It's no accident that we are designed in such a way that we can't fully see ourselves without looking in a mirror! How lucky we are to have millions and billions of mirrors all around us—reflections of our light and our shadows are walking around everywhere to help us see ourselves more fully. We are here to help each other evolve and grow.

Michael Neill, one of the authors we mentioned earlier in the chapter, likes to say, "We are the projector, not the camera." What he means is that we think we are registering facts that have been broadcasted by others—but we're actually projecting assumptions out from ourselves. Everything and everyone is a reflection of your current perception and vibration. Put a different way, you can't see what you are not. You see what you believe.

We are always putting some energy into the field of consciousness and into the soup of humanity, whether we know it or not. Think of someone you admire. Maybe it's a role model, a world leader, a loved one, or a friend. With that person in your mind, think of three qualities you admire about them. Got them?

Those three qualities that you admire in someone else reflect the same qualities that lie within you. You wouldn't be able to admire them unless they were also qualities within you.

The same goes when it comes to our shadows. Think of someone who bugs the shit out of you. For some reason, they are a trigger, and you find yourself irritated or contracted just by thinking of them. Can you feel the stir? Now, think of the three qualities that you don't like about them. Got them? Now, write them down in the margin of this page or in your journal.

Deep breath. You know where this is going . . . You guessed it, those three qualities also exist within you. Those qualities are a part of your shadow. Your shadow is made up of the parts of yourself you don't like or don't want to see.

Often, it's not comfortable to admit that the things that trigger us are also within us. Sometimes, it feels a lot easier and better to blame and judge someone else, rather than asking ourselves why that person bugs us in the first place. Our feelings get stirred up because there is something for us to see and heal. Often, when we don't like something in another person, it is because our feelings are showing us what we value. Usually, we value the opposite of whatever traits or qualities we are judging in others and trying to avoid in ourselves.

JEN'S STORY:

It always drove me crazy when I would witness someone acting like a victim of their circumstances, their day, or their life. My grandmother played this role well. I remember her in her prime—a successful entrepreneur who invented the Ball Boy, the first automatic tennis ball throwing machine, the first sports rebound net to hit the market, and the first group teaching method for the sport. In the 1970s, she was bringing in almost a seven-figure income with her business partner, living on a beautiful 110-acre horse farm in Westchester, New York, and surrounded by abundance in every form you could imagine.

Memories from that time still seem like a fairy tale. Chrissy Evert came to play on our court, fox hunts took place in our meadow, and hunter-jumper horse shows ran in our indoor riding bubble (the largest in the world at the time). I remember the flower gardens, the smell of the greenhouses, and the freedom that the woods would bring. My grandmother was in her highest of highs.

Then, things suddenly changed. My grandparents got divorced, and before I knew it, the farm was sold. Everything I loved on it was gone. In the years that followed, I watched my confident, successful, ambitious grandmother see herself more and more as a victim of her life's circumstances.

I never wanted to be a victim of anything. I didn't value the victim role, nor did I have respect for anyone who embodied it. It sounds harsh, but it is true. The idea of being a victim bugged me, ate at me, and triggered the hell out of me when I saw that trait in another.

Years later, into my adulthood, I was training with teacher and author Debbie Ford and attending her Shadow Workshop in sunny California. I remember her asking me to think of someone I didn't want to be. In that moment, my grandmother came to mind. Debbie asked me why.

"Because she is a victim," I replied.

"What does the opposite of being a victim mean to you?" Debbie probed.

Quiet for a few minutes, I contemplated. And then it hit me. "Being a leader!"

Oh my God, I thought to myself. This is my gift! I've been a leader my whole life. I never even considered that the very thing I didn't want to be was birthing what I would become.

This is the power of the shadow. This is the power of the mirror. What we don't want to see in others is also within us. What we don't want to be is pointing us to who we can become. We really do need each other to see our own light.

Intentionally Trusting Your Light

When we find ourselves lost, confused, or in a low mood, we always have the choice to look to our own light to light the way. But it is indeed a choice, so sometimes we will first look for help from other people and things. This is the trap of the seeker—looking outside of ourselves for the answers, rather than trusting the answers that are always available inside us.

For others, this means stepping inside, retreating to the cave or the ivory tower and trying to solve the "problem" of humanness. This is the trap of the hermit—we look inward for answers that can only be lived through life.

We know these habits all too well. Maybe you do, too. As seekers and strivers, we've been wired to improve. For Jennifer, this has taken the form of going to school; seeking certifications and advanced degrees; working with mediums, healers, and psychics; and going to so many personal and professional development workshops and intensives that she's lost count. Jeff, for his part, has taken the path of the hermit a few too many times, writing endless lists of personal values, goals, and mission statements to try to articulate an ideal instead of dealing with what is right in front of him.

We're not saying that seeking wisdom from others is bad. Thoughtful self-reflection isn't bad either. But what we are saying is that it's sometimes a lot easier to look past our own wisdom to someone who appears to be smarter than us, or to withdraw from the world altogether. Sometimes, the person with the advanced degree doesn't know any better. And other times, there are limits to what you can learn on your own.

With time and age, we've realized that the wisdom that comes from our own light is the most accurate sage, guide, and teacher. It always has our back, no matter how we are feeling in the moment. It is always there waiting for us to trust it, knowing exactly what we need when we need it. It is steadily extending its hand in invitation, ready to guide and light the way. It is available to us through every living moment.

We were reminded of this lesson by Lisa, one of our executive coaching clients. Lisa, an executive director for a community health center, found us when searching the web. She was feeling lost and forgotten to herself, and dealing with a difficult and challenging culture.

After a several months of sessions and attending one of our retreats, Lisa began to have a series of epiphanies. As she began to remember how her inner wisdom used to speak to her, she began to trust her own light more each day. She became more honest with us and herself about what was working for her and what wasn't. We could see and sense a shift taking place—Lisa was beginning to trust her own inner navigational system.

One day, she came to a session with something in her hand. She looked brighter and calmer. Her mood was infectious.

"Guess what I have here?" she said playfully. "This found me last night—it's a journal entry I wrote nearly five years ago."

As we listened, she read it out loud to us. The entry was a conversation between herself and her spirit—in other words, she had written a series of questions and a series of answers from her higher self. We smiled to ourselves, because we love this method of dialogue.

She slowly read the questions and the answers. The questions were deep—fundamental topics like, "Who am I now?"

It was amazing to hear the tone of the answers. They were direct, concise, and wise. "You are who you've always been. You are right where you need to be."

As she revisited her own words, she teared up. When she finished, we were all quiet. She spoke in almost a whisper.

"I had my own answers all along."

Yes! This is exactly what we mean. You can trust the wisdom of your own light.

Creating Space to Trust Your Light

Trusting your light is a choice. It's also an intentional practice. Our light always speaks to us—sometimes in quiet whispers and sometimes with loud commands. Each one of us may experience this dialogue differently. Your light's wisdom may come as a subtle feeling that pulls you in the right direction, or a voice that you come to realize is calling you home. Making space to hear and sense how your light speaks to you is one key to trusting it.

You can create space by scheduling time with yourself to be with yourself. Maybe it feels good to go on a walk or a hike, or meander in the woods or go barefoot on the beach. Or maybe you can take a few moments before you get out of bed in the morning to rest in the dream state you're emerging from before you start your day. Or maybe you do what Lisa did and write a letter to the light within asking questions you want answered—then listen to your own answers.

Your light is always on for you. You can trust that fact.

PRACTICE POINTS

PRACTICING THE SECOND LIGHT
Your Light Is Always On

Practice "I Am"

"I am" is one of the most powerful phrases in the Universe. The words that follow "I am . . ." create your reality, so choose them wisely. When you say "I am tired" or "I am overwhelmed," you've chosen to amplify a feeling that shapes your being. Remember: what you focus on, you feed.

Now, consider the difference between that and when you say "I am supported" or "I am ready." The way we talk to ourselves can be destructive or constructive, depending on what choices we make.

A conscious leader practices the art of manifestation by being consciously aware of how they want to feel—and *be*—in every moment. A conscious leader realizes that moments don't happen to them—moments happen *with* them.

You can practice choice-making with the use of "I am." When you first open your eyes in the morning, take a moment to imagine how you want to feel at the end of your day. Imagine how you want to feel with family and friends. Imagine how you want to feel speaking your truth and shining your light. Imagine how you want to be received by the people you lead.

Imagine how you want to be in relationship with the higher light. Imagine how you want to be right now.

You can use "I am" statements in the morning or any time during the day. We find them most helpful when we first awake or before a meeting, workshop, class, speech, presentation, or conversation. Here are some examples of our "I am" statements that may spark your own.

I am light.

I am present and bring my full presence to wherever I am.

I am aligned to my blueprint and feel purposeful in my actions.

I am connected to my wisdom. I trust my gut, my heart, and my inner knowing.

I am worthy and enough.

I am so grateful for the beauty and bounty all around.

I am right where I need to be.

I am living with vitality, health, and good fortune.

I am supported and guided by each step I take.

I am a magnet for opportunities.

I am blessed with abundance.

I am courageous and capable.

I am helps us tune in and tap into our authentic power. It's a practice that helps us harness the wholeness of who we are as we build alignment with our inner light. It's a powerful tool that elevates our energy field and activates the power of choice that we get to yield as human beings. Go ahead and make up your own!

Use a Mantra

Mantras are a way of combining intention and *I am* statements into a powerful habit. Your words create your experience. Many people have unconscious mantras that repeat often without knowing they are doing so. For example, "I'm too busy," "I don't have time," "I can't do all of this," or "I can't afford it." Imagine replacing these limiting statements with intentional words of power.

Mantras help us clear the space around us and usher in a higher vibration that helps to shift our reality. They are powerful because *you* are powerful. Claiming how you want to be, in whatever words feel natural to you, can help you manifest what you desire. Try it on for size or make up your own mantra. Here are a few we love to use:

- **Releasing Mantra:** "I, _____ [state your name], release, reject, and revoke all contracts, beliefs, programs, and patterns with myself and others that no longer serve my highest and greatest good."

- **Transformation Mantra:** "I bless, uplift, and transform any and all frequency energy and send it back to the Source." (A special thank you to Peggy Black for sharing this mantra.)

- **Grounding Mantra:** "I am fully embodied, anchored to the planet, and divinely supported by Source."

- **Opening Mantra:** "I am calm and confident, and I open my hands and heart to allow other people to be, feel, think, and do whatever they need to be, feel, think, and do."

- **Abundance Mantra:** "I am propelled and protected by the magic of the Universe, which is working on my behalf to create abundance more powerful than I can imagine."

- **Protective Mantra:** "I am in the light, of the light, and I will express the light." This is a powerful mantra Jennifer has used since she was young. It has served her well during her darkest and scariest moments, bringing her protection and alignment to the Divine when needed.

Look for the Light in Another

If you are light, then everyone around you is too. When conversing with someone, look for their light. Instead of focusing on what they say exactly, notice the space they are coming from. Are they distracted? Are they present? Do they feel open or closed? Do they feel tender, or do they feel rigid? What are they wanting you to hear? What does their presence and essence feel like? Notice.

Choose to Close the Distance

When you find yourself disagreeing or having an argument with someone who triggers you, take a moment to create space for yourself. Let it breathe. Sleep on it. Take some time off from having to engage.

If the relationship is important to you and you want that person in your life, close the distance. What we mean by this is take the first step. Pick up the phone. Invite them to lunch. Go for a walk and work it out.

This strategy only works if the other party is interested in closing the distance too. If they are, there is gold in the growth that will come. If not, let it go and allow it to be.

Use Listening and Reflection

Ask and listen more. Talk less. That is the secret to surfacing the wisdom in the room. Your team has the answers you seek. Your community has the insights you need. Your clients have the solutions to your business challenges. You just need to extract them.

When you do listen, practice reflecting back what you heard. Say, "What I hear you saying is . . . Is that accurate?"

This kind of active reflection fosters trust between people, because most of us want to be seen and heard. When you listen, observe, and reflect, you will notice common themes you can use to create common ground.

Surface the Wisdom in the Room

We do a lot of group facilitation in our work. Usually, the compliment we receive is in the result—a group that is more aligned and effective. Occasionally, though, someone will observe our process and ask, "Wow, what is your secret?"

It's a four-step process for surfacing the wisdom in the group and creating alignment. It goes like this:

1. **Get into your heart.** We do something to get people into their hearts and out of their heads. Often, the groups we lead are moving fast, physically and mentally. That's not the right space for accessing new ideas or finding common ground. Usually, we lead a guided meditation. Other times, we ask people to take a few deep breaths, inviting their full presence and attention to arrive in the moment, and sometimes we play a song, show a video, or tell a story that will help our busy-minded audience drop into accessing their full presence.

2. **Silent reflection.** After we do that, we ask a question and give everyone time to answer it on their own (personally and silently).

3. **Small group sharing.** We then ask each person to share their answer (whatever they are comfortable sharing) with four to five people in their pod (a small group), creating intimacy and connection within that small group.

4. **Large group discussion.** Lastly, we bubble up. We ask each pod to share themes or common thoughts that were discussed, so everyone in the room can hear.

You can do this in person or virtually, whatever online meeting platform you use. When you do this, everyone gets to play and participate. The introverts get time to be reflective and safely share with a smaller group. The extroverts get to be the spokespersons. And together, everyone in the room hears what's surfaced, which is a key step to creating alignment. It's easy to do, and it's incredibly effective. Try it!

Look for the Gift

The late Debbie Ford was an amazing author, teacher, and guide. She had an uncanny ability to help her students extract the wisdom in the shadow. We include this powerful practice point in honor of her spirit.

Think of someone who bugs, triggers, or annoys you. Pick one quality you don't like about them. In your journal, write down why that one quality bothers you so much. Do you see that same quality in other people?

Once you have identified the quality and the reason behind why you don't like it, think of its opposite value. What is it? Do you see that quality come to life in yourself? Write down what you notice.

Create Space for Self-Care

We talk all the time with leaders who say that their calendar runs their lives. What happens if you reverse that? What happens if you exert a bit of influence on your calendar?

There is a ton of new research suggesting that the less you work, the more successful you are, but boy, does that go against the norms of modern society, at least in the United States. For us, intentionally creating more space in the work week has been a game-changer in our success. Instead of putting our personal wellbeing in a box as a "nice to have," we've made it into a "must have." We've rearranged our business so we have the capacity to do so, and we can give from a place of fullness.

We started by making changes to our vacation calendar—closing our offices more frequently throughout the year. It's a luxury you can choose as a business owner. We now take a full week off for Thanksgiving, two weeks for the winter holidays, a full week off for the Fourth of July, and long weekends for other holidays. We tack on personal vacations to travel the world or go to our favorite places on top of that, and we alter those as needed so one of us can hold down the fort when the other is away.

We first scheduled "Awesome Hour" each morning to ensure we align our lights to co-lead the day. We then added in "Free Fridays" to the mix, where we shut down our offices at noon every week to ensure everyone in the company, including ourselves, was taking care of themselves and doing whatever they needed to fill up their tanks before the weekend. And lastly, we added Wednesday afternoon study halls as a client-free block of time to get work done.

All of these adjustments helped us get off our own self-induced hamster wheel. We made a choice to fill up and take care of ourselves first, so we can take care of the ones we serve second. It's made all the difference.

Look at your calendar. What space can you make to create more joy, fulfillment, and freedom in your day, week, month, and year? Once you get clear on that, schedule an appointment with yourself and stick to it.

Get Out in Nature

Going outside to breathe the fresh air, walking in the woods, or sitting by the water's shore can help you feel the force field that we are all connected to. It's a natural mood shifter that usually helps us get out of our heads as we allow the healing quality of nature to do its work. Taking a nature bath helps us shift our focus from what's not working to what is. When we do, we are more likely to notice the beauty all around us, as we create a bit more space inside ourselves and outside ourselves for our lights to shine.

Clear Your Space

When you want to tune in to the wisdom within, it's helpful to clear any distortion, distractions, or dense energy that might be within your field. Your field could mean your aura, your physical space, your work environment, or your home. Since everything is energy, clearing your space with intention and command supports your ability to create the highest vibration in your environment, as you consciously choose to tune into your light.

One of the best ways to do this is an ancient Native American tradition called smudging, a practice Jennifer learned as a child. Smudging is a practice in which you burn sage, incense, or dried plants (such as white sage, mountain sage or palo santo—a cedar type of wood) and use the smoke with your intention to clear, uplift, and bless an area. You can find smudge sticks almost everywhere, and they are also easy to make on your own if you live out west.

Open the windows of the room you want to clear, center yourself, light the smudge stick, and then walk around to the doors and inside perimeter in a clockwise position. As you walk, set your intention to bring in positive energy and command that any stuck, stagnant, or dense energy leave.

It is helpful to be intentional about your doorways, as they often serve as portals of energy. You can choose what the frequency of that energy is for your clients, teammates, family, friends, or guests when they walk through. We often command peace, love, harmony, and healing to come into these portals. We do this before and after every workshop in our retreat center, at every change of season in our homes, and especially after we entertain.

Follow these steps as a guide, trusting that however you're inspired to do it is perfect.

1.   Open your windows and set the scene by turning on some peaceful music.

2.   Light your smudge stick or palo santo. Blow out the flame after it has burned a little bit, and let it begin to smoke.

3.   First, cleanse yourself by moving the burning herbs or incense around your body, going either from bottom

to top or top to bottom. Make sure you cleanse both your front and your back, as well.

4. Next, move to your front door, but don't open it yet. Face outward and call in your guides, spirit, angels, ancestors, God, Divine Intelligence, Higher Power, nature, ascended masters, or whatever you believe in. Ask them to help you clean and clear you space.

5. Once you've done that, still facing your front door, move the smoke clockwise and use it to trace the outline of your doorway.

6. Next, open the door and make a wide circle toward the ground. You can go either clockwise (for grounding) or counterclockwise (for opening), depending on how you want your guests and family to feel when they enter.

7. Begin to move around the space, tracing the outline of each room from corner to corner. You can wave the smoke over the furniture as well, setting the intention to cleanse the spaces where people sit of their residual energies.

8. Follow your heart as to where you should go and allow the smoke to clear away any stuck or dense energy. You may want to spend a little more time in bathrooms and closets, where denser energy can hide. Also, if you are doing this ritual at home, make sure to cleanse your bedrooms, and especially to spread the smoke over and under your bed.

9. When you are done, extinguish the smudge stick by submerging it in soil or in water.

10. Take note of how you feel afterward and for days to come.

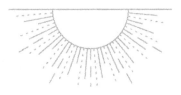

CHAPTER 6

The Third Light

You Only Have to See
What's Right in Front of You

Imagine for a moment that you are walking alone through the woods at dusk. You've been walking at a pretty good pace, but as the sun dips beneath the horizon, it's getting harder and harder to see the path. You slowly make your way a bit further, until you come to a fork in the trail.

You squint around in the dim light and realize you aren't sure where you are anymore.

You're lost.

You put your backpack down and rummage through it to find the lantern you had packed before you left. Time to shine some light on the subject!

As you turn on the lantern, it begins to illuminate the darkness around you. You stand there in gratitude for the glow and lift the lantern slowly over your head. The lantern only illuminates a space of about ten feet around you—not one hundred feet, not one thousand feet, and certainly not miles and miles. Although the lantern only reveals what is right around you, that's all you need to make out a small sign posted at the fork. You haven't been on this stretch of path before, but now at least you know which direction you need to take.

You continue walking with the lantern above your head, more safely, more confidently, and more peacefully.

The Consistency of Change

When we teach the first two Lights of Conscious Leadership—leadership is about first acknowledging that you are a light, and second, that our light is always available to us no matter if we're feeling confident or insecure—we watch our clients go through a similar conversation in their minds. The First Light seems understandable, easy to grasp and apply—especially for those who believe we are more than our bodies and mind. The Second Light is a bit deeper and kinder, in a way, inviting us to let go of the self-induced stress that we all too commonly place on ourselves.

But inevitably, we get one particular question: "I know I have strengths that help people. And I know I can be too hard on myself. But what happens in times when I simply don't *know* what to do next? Everyone is looking to me for the answers. But things are changing so fast, and often I feel lost about what I should do next, let alone about what to tell my team."

Time and again, we run into the false perception that leadership requires being infallible. Many people perceive great leaders to possess such passion and vision that they move determinedly and doggedly in a straight line, climbing over obstacles and never pausing for the slightest indecision. It's a perception that's reinforced by many business books and movies, in which we see the heroine or hero portrayed as an iconic force who bends people and circumstances to their will.

If only it were that easy! Consider this: Have you ever written a strategic plan that anticipated every variable? Have you ever reached a goal in a way where everything went exactly as you thought it would?

Or have you ever achieved a dream, only to look back and say, "It's a miracle I got here at all"?

We want to think of life as a linear progression. But really, change is the only constant in our lives. Change is the natural state of our existence. And change is a curvy, windy road.

If we pay attention, we can observe evidence of change all around us and within us. In nature, we recognize change as the natural process of evolution, and we expect it. We see it in the growth of a caterpillar that miraculously turns into a butterfly, or a garden of seeds planted in soil blooming into nutrient-dense food that nourishes us, or the leaves of Aspen trees that turn from green in summer's shimmering light to golden yellow in the fall.

If we look within, we see that we are constantly changing, too. Our cells regenerate, our skin sheds and renews, and our hair turns gray (or we lose it altogether) as we age. How we see and view the world changes as well, as we continuously forge new neuropathways in our brain with the thoughts and behaviors we cycle through.

Change is vitally important for our individual and collective evolution.

Looking back, you can probably see how both big and small changes have impacted your life. Often, some of the most significant events in our lives are not part of our plan. They seem to come out of the blue—and when they do, we learn to adapt and respond. We learn to acclimate to a new normal with patience and courage. We learn to harness the natural resilience we're all born with.

And yet, so much of leadership and life seems to revolve around planning rather than presence—looking ahead to the possible forks in the path, instead of minding the trail under our feet. Looking forward to our first job, only to land into a career we never imagined; spending days on a strategic plan that becomes obsolete a month into the new year; or putting off a relationship to earn a living, only to meet a future spouse by chance. We fool ourselves into thinking that our lives take a linear path, when the evidence all around us shows that they are full of twists and turns.

So, why do we put so much pressure on ourselves to know what's coming? Are we too afraid to trust ourselves to know what to do in the moment? Are we too skeptical to trust that everything will work out for the best?

Why do we spend so much time looking to the horizon when the stuff that matters is often right under our feet?

The Third Light of Conscious Leadership points us back to the here and now. We don't have to see ahead to the weeks, months, and years before us. And actually, we can't. All we can see are the cues around us that inform our next few steps. If we make each next step with awareness, alignment, and intention, then each next step will lead us further down the path we need to travel.

Think about it: If you look back on your life, can you see how your yellow brick road was perfectly paved—brick by brick—to lead you to who you've become today? We're not suggesting it was all easy, or that you'd want to live it over again. But can you see how every twist and turn, fit and start, success and failure, and experience of love and loss got you to the beautiful being you are right now? Your past experiences help shape the person you are today.

What if that same yellow brick road was winding out in front of you, too?

What if the changes that seem so unsettling in the moment are the exact experiences you need to help you reach your dreams?

If you can see the perfect design of your path and yellow brick road in the past, then you can trust that it is being laid out for your future. Conscious leaders trust the light of the present. We all have a choice.

We can choose to take the pressure off ourselves and trust that we are right where we need to be. We can listen to the intelligence within our own light, rather than ignoring it. We can loosen our grip on the need to predict the future, and instead become the master of creating it.

The Most Successful Quarter Yet

It was late February 2020, and our team was sitting together in HeartSpace to tackle a huge problem: we had too much work scheduled. A few large-scale organizations had reached out, almost simultaneously, for strategic planning help—and all the deals had closed. For a day, we were all excited as we looked ahead to a record quarter.

Then the reality dawned on us. How were we going to do it all?

There was the marketing agency in Toronto that needed an in-person culture reboot—the week before a major Miami hospital needed to kick off concept development for a new fundraising campaign. There was a national alcohol spirits brand in Chicago that wanted a strategic kickoff during the same week that a family foundation in San Francisco wanted a private, closed-door strategy session for high-net-worth investors.

How many flights was this going to take?

We spent the better part of a week looking at timelines, adjusting calendars, and swapping around dates and times with all the clients and our families. By early March, we had a way to make it work. It was going to be busy, but we could do it. A couple of times we were worried that one of the clients was going to drop, but we managed to herd the cats into an elegant solution. Our plan was flawless, and Q2 2020 was going to be our most successful yet.

Well, you know what happened next. We never implemented our flawless plan. A week after we locked in the details, we all literally got locked in ourselves, as the pandemic reached a critical point in the United States. Our schedules, packed to the gills with wall-to-wall discovery sessions and kickoff meetings only one week before, were wiped laughably clean.

In fact, we never ended up doing one minute of work with any of those clients. And we never ended up receiving one dollar, either. All the clients canceled. Q2 2020 would become a financial mess.

But looking back, in a strange way, we were right that it was also our most successful yet. With no clients and free calendars, we started talking about how to use the time productively. Who did we want to be? We knew that the Plenty way was to help. How could we help?

Jen had the idea that we could create a "Coronacare" community to help people find support online. Jeff created data dashboards to help people understand what was happening. Sierra created inspirational content and posts. Bryan helped us create a podcast. By late March, long before there were daily graphs on every major news outlet and online support groups in every corner of the internet, Plenty had set up ways to educate, support, and care for our people.

It wasn't seamless, or easy—a few times our team members had to say, "Slow down! We're moving too fast." But bit by bit, we followed what was in front of us. We set an intention to help, did our best to let go of financial worries, and started walking.

Bringing Awareness to the Here and Now

We may think that we can see what our lives will be like in a decade, a year, a month, a week, a day, an hour from now. But the truth is, those are projections—hopes, dreams, fears, goals, and wishes for what might be on the path in front of us. Just like a lantern in our hand only illuminates the darkness directly around us, all we really know is right here, right now.

Now, if you can only see what is right in front and around you, what do you notice? What signs are being illuminated? Do you see something that sparks your curiosity? Do you feel drawn toward an idea? Do you hear something? Do you notice clues about what direction to take? We bet you do.

When you follow the cues, they inform what step you should take next. And when you take that next step, guess what happens? The lantern light comes with you, illuminating once again what's right around you from that new place in time. When you combine the light with your full presence—being completely present in the current moment—you notice what's showing up. You notice how your body feels with what is showing up as it interacts with the clues that are coming in. And every time you "show up to what shows up," as our dear friend Scott Kelly says, you are given the inner wisdom that helps you take the next step. That inner wisdom is your very own navigation system—always on and always available to help you lead and live the life you desire.

You see, you really don't need to see three years out—or one year, for that matter. Too many conditions are likely to change that you just can't control nor predict. *What you can control is what you see, sense, feel, and know to be true in the present moment.* When you harness that ability, you become your own guide. All that is required is for you to be as present as possible to notice as much as possible. For when you are fully here in the moment, you become more fully embodied in the present. You see more signs, you hear more of the symphony, you feel more synchronicities, and you notice more connections in the mysterious force field that unites us all.

Leading and living this way takes the pressure off. You drop the need to figure things out. You loosen your grip and need to control your future and the people in it. You become less stressed and feel freer as you get curious about what you see. You become more trusting that the Universe has your back and knows exactly what you need when—and you become more trusting of your own ability to navigate whatever comes your way. You become pleasantly mystified about how it all works as you practice the art of presence, which helps to lay down your bricks in perfect, divine order on your unique yellow brick road.

JEN'S STORY:

In 2015, I was securing funding for one of my previous companies, Healthy Happy Human Beings. My office consisted of two rooms in the back of a beautiful building at the base of Park City Mountain Resort, conveniently located just two miles from my home. A part of my business plan was to create a wellbeing retreat center.

In my office, there was a door that was always closed. It led to some mysterious space at the front of the building. For almost five years, I'd pass it by daily, almost without thinking about it. One day I suddenly began to notice something when I passed by the door. It began to pull at me. It was almost as if there was a whisper that came through it, saying, "Open me!"

The voice became too strong to ignore. When I opened the door, I was awestruck. It was perfect! Fourteen hundred square feet of a large open room with beautiful windows and light, accompanied by a welcoming entrance with gorgeous wood accents. I knew this was the place I was meant to expand into. And, with some investigating, I learned it was so open because the current tenant was getting ready to vacate the building and move out!

Thrilled, I contacted my landlord and began the process of negotiation. I knew I had to secure it, but I had no idea how I would pay for it or make it happen.

Over the weeks that followed everything seemed to unfold like a fairytale.

I met the landlord's various requirements. While this was happening, Jeff and I decided to merge our work. We named the new space HeartSpace, and together we decorated her with cozy couches, plush rugs, conversational pods, and a bar. We wanted HeartSpace to be an "unconference space" that would provide a safe, trusting, and connective environment for our clients to enjoy.

We were intentional about everything—writing positive affirmations on every wall before they were to be painted, pouring high-vibration essential oils of "joy," "abundance," and "peace" into the paint to cover the walls.

As we built out HeartSpace, a hotel thirty yards away was built out too. It just so happened to be the perfect place for our out-of-town clients to stay. Then one day, while sitting on the couches with our team, I made a fist with my right

*hand and punched the open palm of my left and said out
loud, "Now, all we need is a path to get from HeartSpace
to the beautiful hiking trails that surround us!"*

*We took a break, and when we went outside onto the back
terrace, we saw a bulldozer paving a path from HeartSpace
to the trails, just as I had commanded moments before!*

*For eight years now, we've welcomed thousands of conscious
leaders from around the globe, from companies like
Jim Beam, Wounded Warrior Project, March of Dimes,
Cruzan Rum, Hornitos Tequila, Blue Bunny Ice Cream,
and Maker's Mark, as well as the former senator and US
ambassador to China Max Baucus and the Horton Group,
into our HeartSpace home. Their passions, purpose, and
dreams for a better world have left a vibrational imprint
on the walls, and their photographs remind me of the
yellow brick road that has been perfectly paved for us.*

The story of HeartSpace is another example of what happens
when you put the metaphorical lantern over your head. The
light shines on what is right around you, and when you are
paying attention, you notice clues. When you act on what you
notice, you begin to follow the breadcrumbs of life with more
ease and wonder. You realize that you have to expend less effort,
because somehow, whatever you need shows up exactly when
you need it to! The friend who calls when you need some support, the hummingbird that flies in front of you only to pause
in midair to make sure you see it, the words from a colleague
that touch your soul and lead to a new job opportunity. These

moments happen all the time, showing up to help guide our next steps.

What would happen if you chose to see that everything was connected? What would happen if you only had to pay attention to the very next step? Would you trust more? Relax more? Let go more?

This is the invitation of the lantern—it helps free up your control on the future so you can allow life to work through you, rather than you having to work at life. This is what's on offer when you commit to noticing what's right around you and simply taking the next step.

Aligning to What's Next

Once you bring your full awareness to the present and notice what is showing up, you can consciously choose what to do with the information you take in. Is there something to do? Is there something not to do? Is there something to say?

Unfortunately, there's no one who will be able to tell you what choices to make. There's no instruction manual that will tell you either. That's because no one is exactly like you. No one is in your exact shoes. And no one can see, sense, and feel what you do. Except you!

So how do you know what choice is best? How do you align with your light to take the next step?

The first answer lies in this: *Be your own lantern.*

If you are light, and your light is always on, then it really doesn't matter what happens to you. If you are paying attention, you will always be given information in some form as to how best to respond to the current situation.

You don't need the government, a doctor, or a teacher to tell you what's best for you. Obviously, sometimes it doesn't hurt to seek help and guidance—we all need experts to help us from time to time. But you have a navigational guidance system within you, too. That guidance system is your light, showing you the way. And, that light, the light within you, knows exactly what you need, what you want, and what is best for you.

How?

Look for the landing. What we mean by this is when you are in a situation, try and take in as much information as possible. Don't do anything while you notice what you notice. Listen for your own certainty. If you don't get a hit right away about what to do (or not do), wait. If you are deliberating, hemming, hawing, and weighing options, wait. "Convincing yourself" is different from "knowing."

Give yourself time and space to watch and wait for the insight, clarity, and direction to land. It might happen right away. Or it might not—sometimes the best strategy is to leave things alone for a while. That said, you might get the urge to pick up the phone and call someone. You might feel clear about saying "yes" or "no" to whatever appears. Whatever "it" is, give yourself the time you need to respond as you allow yourself to know when you know.

But how will you know when you know? That answer is different for everyone, but it's perhaps the most important skill to learn. For some, knowing comes from conviction and a certainty of belief. For others, knowing rises up as a visceral reaction like getting goosebumps. Jennifer gets a strong, full-body knowing—a sensation that is clear, confident, and unwavering. For Jeff, knowing comes in the form of a calm certainty—when the mental gymnastics, scenario planning, and rationalization slow down, he knows that he knows.

Knowing when you know, without having to know how you know, is one of the greatest tools conscious leaders can use to align to their light. We call it "looking for the landing." Here are some steps that may be helpful:

Notice what shows up in your field: What do you see? What do you sense? What do you feel?

Investigate the cues: Notice where your attention is drawn. Look up the symbolic meaning of the animal that just crossed your path (such as "What is the spiritual meaning of the hummingbird?"), ask for more information in the conversation you are in, reflect back to someone what you are hearing, and listen to your body's sensations!

Create space to sense the landing: Go for a walk, change the subject, or take your attention off the matter at hand.

Trust your knowing, then act.

Knowing When to Act

JEN'S STORY:

It was an early summer day, and I was packing up our trailer to head out on a camping trip with friends, when the phone rang. It was my son Riley calling from our neighborhood park.

"Mom, I think I broke my leg."

"I'll be right there," I responded and hung up the phone and got my husband, Kristian, to get in the car with me.

When we showed up, we were stunned to see Riley on the ground with his whole right leg already black and blue. He couldn't move his foot. He was in shock, and although I couldn't see it at the time, so was I. Literally and figuratively, a traumatic experience came out of the blue that would change the trajectory of our lives.

Riley had been play wrestling with a boy much heavier than he was. As they wrestled, all of the body weight of the boy landed on Riley's leg, tearing every muscle and tendon in his knee. The worst part was that his peroneal nerve (the nerve that controls the flexing of the foot) was damaged upon impact, leaving him unable to move his foot, a condition known as foot drop.

The impact was severe, not only to his physical body, but to his mental and emotional being—and to mine, too. What would happen to my gifted athlete? Would he ever be able to walk normally again? Would he ever be able to return to the lacrosse field? Would he ever be able ride his skateboard or ski down a mountain? The prognosis did not look good.

A month following the accident, Riley underwent successful reconstructive orthopedic surgery. Doctors repaired the torn muscles and tendons in his knee, but told us we would have to wait and pray that the peroneal nerve would eventually wake up on its own. The waiting was nerve-racking (pun intended). Every day, no movement. Every test, no signal. Every month that passed by, no response.

As we waited for something to shift, I felt like we were in a ticking time bomb. We were told by several doctors that if the muscles in his lower leg did not receive the nerve impulses from a wakeful and working nerve, the muscles would eventually turn to tissue, and he would never regain foot motion.

Seven months passed, and despite my natural optimistic state, my worry and restlessness began to noticeably increase. I can't explain the feeling, but I liken it to a horse in a stall that suddenly perks its ears and lifts its hooves as it picks up on the subtle energy of a thunderstorm coming. That is the sensation I had in my body—the sensation that I had to move and do something, the sensation that we could not wait a single moment longer. I just knew I had to do something. I knew I had to find a solution and that it was time to act.

And that's what I did. I began my search for a specialized nerve surgeon who could help. I asked friends who put me in touch with phenomenal doctors around the country. My husband and I got educated and heard over and over that there was no good solution to reversing foot drop.

Through a series of synchronicities and miracles, we got connected to an incredible resource called the Health Network Foundation, which helped put our story out to the most respected hospitals in the country. And within two weeks, I got the call I was praying for. It was from Dr. Mitchel Seruya, a neurosurgeon at Cedar Sinai Hospital in Los Angeles. After thirty minutes of conversation late at night, Kristian and I knew he was our guy. We had surgery scheduled before we hung up.

Riley underwent a pioneering surgery that literally rewired his right leg. Dr. Seruya took his toe nerve and attached it to the muscles in Riley's lower leg, allowing him to move his foot once more. It was an absolute miracle!

A few months after that, Riley returned to the lacrosse field. With each game, he gained more confidence in his body, strength in his mind, deftness in his skill, and determination in his outlook. The seasons that followed unfolded like a fairy tale. He won two state championships, became all-state, and was the second-highest scorer on his team. He just graduated from high school and will head off to San Diego State University in the fall, where he will play lacrosse and study neuroscience, an area of interest birthed from his journey.

In hindsight, I knew the moment it was time to act—when patience was no longer the path to pursue. My body gave me clear signals to know I had to do something, and I listened.

How do you know when you know?

The Role of Planning

When we introduce the Third Light of Conscious Leadership, You Only Need to See What's Right in Front of You, at our retreats, we watch as the leaders in attendance look both simultaneously relieved and confused. The relief comes from understanding that a leader doesn't have to be infallible. After all, if the future were certain, we wouldn't need leaders to light the way. The concept that "you only have to see what is right in front of you" takes the pressure off, ironically allowing for more freedom to make better decisions.

But the confusion comes in with the idea of planning. So many of us have learned that leadership and teamwork are about planning. We are often asked, "Do we get rid of planning?"

We strongly believe in planning, goal setting, visioning, and forecasting. But those are *process* tools designed to help us *align* with our team members—not crystal balls designed to predict the future. In other words, the *process* of inclusive, thoughtful, rigorous planning is the end in and of itself, because it builds connection, coherence, alignment, and community. The error in planning is not in doing it—the error is in not doing it collaboratively and then expecting the plans will work as you wrote them. They won't.

By all means, plan—but we'd advise you to spend less time preparing the PowerPoint and more time being present with the conversation.

Intentionally Taking the Next Step

When you place the lantern over your head, it illuminates what's right around you in the present moment. You can reflect on where you've been and imagine where you might go, but ultimately, you'll be called back to the present of the light's glow.

What is the lantern illuminating now? You'll realize you can let go of your past regrets, failures, and mistakes, and realize that you can rewrite what you imagine your future to be. When you practice being present to what you observe here and now, you will notice signs and synchronicities that come in from all directions. Then, you can choose whether to follow them or not.

What would be on offer if you could trust that there are no accidents? How would you live and lead if you experienced the connection in everything? What would happen if you genuinely felt you were guided and held in every moment, every step of the way?

This is the invitation of the light. All we must do is take one step at a time. And when we take a step, the light of the lantern and the light within us illuminates the next step, and then the next. Before we know it, our yellow brick road has been laid not only for us, but by us, as we step into the conscious leaders we were always meant to be.

Living this way brings us into a deeper sense of peace and freedom. We take the self-induced pressure off ourselves and release the need to figure everything out. We check in with ourselves to see what direction and steps feel best. We start to make more intentional choices that empower us. We start to say "no" to things that don't feel good, and we start to say "yes" to things that do. Each time we do, we empower ourselves by stepping into the light that we are, and we begin to model the way for others to do the same.

In the end, once we start taking life step by step, we open ourselves to the possibility in the fourth light—that there's a benevolent force all around us, working on our behalf.

PRACTICE POINTS

PRACTICING THE THIRD LIGHT

You Only Have to See

What Is Right in Front of You

Honor the Steps You've Already Taken

To get to the beautiful being that you are right now, you've clearly taken a lot of steps (and even leaps). Your entire life has been made up of putting one foot in front of the other. You know how to do it, and you've done it well. Why not take a moment to celebrate and honor the steps you've already taken?

Take a moment to scan over the choice points of your life.

When were you at a crossroads?

When did you have to leap?

When did you make amends?

When did you ask for help?

When did you choose to leave the nest?

When did you choose to visit a new place?

What happened when you made these choices? Where did these courageous steps lead you?

After you've brought awareness to the steps you've taken in the past, honor them with gratitude. Write a gratitude letter to yourself.

Make a List of What's Right Around You

What choice points, tasks, projects, or to-dos feel present to you right now? Allow your thoughts to meander between personal and professional subjects. Get your answers down on paper.

Then look at your list and investigate what feels best in the moment. Circle the items where you feel open, expanded, and leaning. Notice the ones you didn't circle, too. Then, looking at your day, pick two or three items that you can choose to complete. Set your intention on how you want to feel when they are completed (remember, imagine the task is complete, and bring that feeling into your body as if that completeness is happening in the present).

Follow The Path of Least Resistance

Bring awareness to the current that is always flowing within and around you.

- Press the easy button.

- Notice where the momentum is and ride it.

- Bring more attention to where you feel inspired, and do more of that.

- Say "no" to anything that feels off, hard, or a struggle.

Listen to the Whispers

These subtle nudges and cues are always around us, and they come in from multiple directions. We can see and hear them if we are present and paying attention. Instead of recognizing them in hindsight (when they are most clear), challenge yourself to notice them now—before you, beside you, and around you.

Do your best not to dismiss them as random happenstance. Take note, literally. A great way to do this is right before you go to bed. Grab your journal (or device of choice) and write down what whispers wanted your attention today. Take inventory.

Do this every day for a week. On the seventh day, read your inventory and see if there are any patterns that jump out to you.

Pay Attention to the Angel Escorts

People come in and out of our lives for important reasons. Some teach us, some challenge us, some love us, and some escort us. Scan your life and take a moment to acknowledge the people who have entered (and possibly exited) that have helped you learn, grow, and evolve. Was there a past boyfriend or girlfriend? A mentor? An employee? A boss? Was it some stranger you sat next to on an airplane? Who escorted you to become a better version of yourself?

"Show Up to What Shows Up"

This is one of our favorite lines, courtesy of our friend and colleague Scott Kelly. To us, it's a short, catchy phrase that invites us to fully meet whatever is meeting us. It serves as a grand invitation to trust that we have everything we need at the moment to respond to whatever greets us. It helps us drop the need and pressure to plan and predict, and creates space for us to simply be.

When you lift the lantern over your head, what does it illuminate?

Who comes into your field? Who calls you? Who asks for your time and attention?

What invitations emerge?

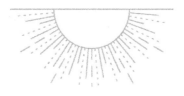

CHAPTER 7

The Fourth Light
There's a Larger Light Guiding You

Take a moment to settle and become still.

Find a comfortable and quiet place to sit with your feet on the ground and your back supported. Close your eyes and draw your attention inward. Notice your breath, this gift of life you have been given. Simply observe the natural rhythm of your inhale and exhale as you bring your full attention to this present moment.

As you look inward, imagine you can see and sense your inner light rising like the sun above the horizon. Feel the warmth of the rays as your inner light becomes brighter and warmer, radiating from the inside out. This light calms you and relaxes you, as the heat melts any tension away. Your shoulders begin to drop, your legs let go, and your belly expands as your light shines throughout your body and beyond.

Imagine your inner light expanding beyond the bounds of your physical structure and into the air and space around you. The rays grow stronger, and your illumination shines brighter as your inner light travels throughout your home or workplace, your community, state, country, planet, and beyond. Your inner light begins to travel out into space and out through multiple galaxies finding its way to the Source—whatever you imagine that to be. Your inner light connects with the higher light. You are bonded and part of something greater—a benevolent force that unites all living species and all sentient beings. You feel peace as you bathe in the light you are, the light you that you are a part of, and the light that shines upon you.

With intention, ask or imagine that the light from the Source guides you on your path today. Ask for help. Ask for what you need at this moment. Maybe it's a question you are seeking an answer to. Maybe it's a challenge you need a solution to. Maybe you need a clear and obvious sign to remind you that you are not alone. Ask your higher light to be present with you today, to work through you, guide you, and help you along your path.

Feel the light from Source, God, Goddesses, the Universe, and Nature flow in and through you now. Feel your awareness expand. Feel your mind calm. Feel your heart open. Feel your body enliven.

Then, gently bring your awareness back to your breath, noticing the depth of your inhalation and exhalation. Notice the furniture you sit on and how you feel supported by it in this moment. Notice the quality of the air around you. And, when you are ready, gently open your eyes.

Welcome back. Feel free to journal or take note of what you experienced in the margins of these pages.

Are We There Yet?

During our workshops and retreats, we use nature and the outdoors to help our attendees connect to the higher light. We do a lot of our work in Park City, Utah—one of the best backyards in the country, it offers us a huge variety of trails, venues, and vistas to enjoy.

Last summer, we took one of our groups out for a mountain walk. The weather was hot and dry—typical mountain desert climate. That weather and Park City's elevation made the walk more challenging than we intended, particularly for the attendees from the East Coast and the Midwest who weren't used to the altitude. The group got pretty strung out along the trail, and we had to keep a careful watch on people to make sure they were drinking enough water and taking their time.

For the first fifteen minutes or so, the group talked and laughed. We heard a lot of people imitating kids in the back seat: "Are we there yet?"

But we noticed that as people got more tired, they quieted down. They stopped wondering where they were going, or how much longer it would take. They stopped asking us where we were headed and pulled their view from the mountain landscapes to their feet.

When we got to the clearing at the top of the trail, we noticed every person doing the same thing. As they gradually came to a halt, everyone would look around and inhale the magnificent view. "Wow," they'd say. And then, to a person, each would look back toward our cars in the parking lot, which now looked tiny from our vantage point. "I can't believe how high we climbed in such a short walk!"

Trusting the Guide

When you're walking up a new mountain path, everything seems easier if you have a guide with you who has been there before.

Life is the same way. It's much easier to take the next step when you trust that something greater than yourself is walking with you. Even when everything seems dark, you're never truly alone.

The Fourth Light of Conscious Leadership speaks to just that—the idea that as we walk our path, there's a larger light guiding us. We are never truly alone.

Call it God, Goddess, Spirit, the Universe, Divine Intelligence, or Jesus Christ. Call it Christ Consciousness, Buddha, Nature, Fate, or Source. Call it Evolution, Math, or Science. Whatever you name it to be, we believe there is a larger light guiding the world around us, in a way that brings order and structure out of entropy. We believe this light is intelligent, benevolent, and good.

When we introduce this fourth light at our retreat, we do our best to clarify that we're not asking anyone to subscribe to a certain set of spiritual or religious beliefs. What we are pointing to is the fact that there's a huge universe out there, and it turns out it doesn't revolve around us. In our modern society, we've done such a good job of planning and building our world that we forget that the world—Nature, the Universe, the larger light—is the architect. The sun rises and sets on its own, without you having to set an phone alarm. The seasons change without you scheduling a video conference to make it happen. Billions of people live, love, laugh, cry, and die all around the world—and you are a part of that majesty.

As confusing and chaotic as our personal lives can sometimes seem, there's an underlying structure to things. If you consider yourself a devout Christian, your structure may have a strong religious component. If you consider yourself a rational scientist, your worldview may not incorporate a deity, but it has no less of an underlying structure. Whether you believe the Universe was created out of God's love, from the infinite density of a tiny point expanding in an instant, or any one of countless other beliefs people hold, there's some level at which your structure explains things for you that you can't see or directly prove.

This higher intelligence—this larger light, as we like to call it—is everywhere and in every living thing. It doesn't matter what gender we identify as, what country we were born into, what belief system we resonate with, or what color our skin may be. We all come from the same source—and we are all connected to it.

Look back on your life. Have you ever experienced a connection with something bigger than yourself? Perhaps in a dark moment, you experienced a feeling of a higher presence that helped you through trouble in the past? Or perhaps there was a time you felt completely alone and lost, only to emerge from your circumstances so grateful that such a painful stretch became foundational for your growth and learning?

Perhaps you experienced it in a place of worship, as a deep, unknowing faith. Or perhaps it came to you in academics as a serene confidence in your abilities. Maybe you experienced a kind of supernatural flow on the athletic field. Maybe you experienced an unexplainable and deep connection with a stranger. We'd say that each of those are experiences with the larger light we're talking about.

You may have learned a certain way to connect with the larger light. Or, you may have learned to commune with a higher source in your own unique way from your lived experiences. Light is experienced in many ways. For some people, the divine hand of God/Goddess has ushered in a life-changing awakening through direct experience. An increasing number of others have experienced light in moments characterized as near death experiences (NDEs)—near death experiences, during which they are literally pronounced physically dead for several minutes and have a mystical experience on the other side, only to wake back up in their bodies.

Others talk of being swept up in divine inspiration creating music or art, literally feeling one with the higher light as the muse works through them.

Others have lived through "in the basement" moments: While crying on the bathroom floor or lying in a hospital bed, lost in low-quality thinking, hopelessness, despair, sadness, or grief, millions of people just like you have been suddenly greeted with the grace of a higher light when they needed it most.

Wouldn't it be healthier and easier if we didn't have to get to our lowest of lows or rarest moments of achievement to realize that we are always supported and guided?

We believe light is everywhere and in every living thing. A higher light is always with you because it's also *in* you. It has our backs and wants the very best for us and from us. Born of a thousand names, its identity changes depending on what we believe, how we grew up, our cultural conditioning, and what religious or spiritual associations we have been a part of.

What would happen if you acknowledged your higher light and intentionally built a relationship with it in work and life?

Being Aware of a Larger Light

JEFF'S STORY:

In chapter 2, I talked a bit about my dad's death and the months of confusion and loss I felt as I tried to sort through a life that felt painful and pointless. I've known people who have found comfort in God during troubled times, but at least in that period of my life, I didn't want to have anything to do with Light, Spirit, God, the Divine, or any other name for it, thank you very much. I was angry and sad, and my only solace seemed to come from hanging onto those emotions.

As I started to take ownership of those feelings, though, I began to notice some subtle changes. It wasn't groundbreaking, at least at first, but it was noticeable. The first thing I noticed one day was the absence of anger. I woke up, pulled myself out of bed to get ready for work, and as I drank some morning coffee, I found myself smiling at one of my small kids playing in the living room.

"Wow," I realized. "I just smiled." Holy smokes, I'm not angry at the world. "My kids are so lovely," I thought. "Dad would be proud."

Little by little, dark things started to drop away. Not all at once, and not in a straight line. But I started to be able to piece together a couple of good days in a row. And as I noticed that, I noticed it was easier to find things that seemed funny and joyful and beautiful.

That same summer, my wife Jeanie and I started to have a discussion about our house. The quiet lake cottage, that was the dream with two kids, was overflowing with four. I had a sense that she had wanted to discuss it for a while but had held back for fear of overwhelming me, too.

Something in me clicked with the idea. As a family, we were ready—and for myself, I could see how much I needed a fresh start, a place where I could be intentional about the next set of memories I made. A place that didn't have constant reminders of my dad. I recalled a house we had seen a few years ago. "That house would be so perfect for our family," Jeanie said. "But there's no way it's still on the market."

Somehow, I knew. I went over to the computer, did a quick search, and there it was. We closed on it a week or so later.

A few months later, we were moving into the house. Boxes were literally everywhere, and our young kids played in them as we slowly put together our new home. As I was unpacking dishes in the kitchen, I looked out the back windows, into the woods behind our house. A huge, magnificent buck stood there on the crest of the hill, only thirty yards away. I waited for him to start and run away, but to my surprise, he slowly walked toward me instead. He looked me right in the eye for a few moments, and then quietly turned to disappear in the woods.

I can't tell you how, but I felt it was the light of my father. I felt that he was okay—and that he wanted me to be okay, too. No, not okay—he wanted me to be full of joy.

We believe the larger light wants to inspire us—to be "in spirit"—and work through us to help us realize our potential and live our purpose. It wants to play. It wants to help and is always there to offer a guiding, supportive hand. Harnessing our conscious leadership powers, we can intentionally invite the higher light in. When we practice this ourselves, we're always in awe of what it transforms—a difficult conversation resolves with understanding and agreement, an unseen solution emerges from out of nowhere, or a challenging employee decides to leave on their own. Could it really be this easy to get this kind of help?

The Source of Your Superpower

We met Timothy about seven years ago at one of our first Lantern sessions. A successful educator, Timothy had a PhD, had a job as a senior executive at a nonprofit, and was starting a second career as a leadership professor. Not surprisingly given his background and profession, he was exceedingly smart, articulate, and thoughtful. He seemed sure of himself and his path.

As is almost always the case with the people who come to Lantern, Timothy already seemed to have everything figured out. He clearly loved his career, and if the way he carried himself at the retreat was any indication, he was great at it. And there was something about him—a bit of a spark. He had a charisma that gave off a feeling of positivity. It was hard to describe, but we could feel it.

When we went around the room the first night and asked everyone to share why they were here, Timothy's response sounded like the response of a professor. "I'm always seeking to sharpen my skills," he shared. "I'd like to keep getting smarter at what I am doing."

He started to change in the small group discussions, though. As he settled in with his group, his tone got less polished and more personal. Not less confident, but way more familiar. He leaned in as his partners talked. We could see something that complemented his intellect: his care. It's a great trait for a teacher, we remarked to each other.

Timothy's breakthrough happened on the second day. We had asked all the participants to draw—a helpful technique to get people out of their overly analytical minds—and specifically, to draw a picture of the best version of themselves. Timothy's picture was a large brain, with lightning bolts coming out of it. "At my best, I spark creativity and insight in others," he explained.

As he talked, one of his fellow group members walked over to his picture with a red marker. As Timothy looked on a bit incredulously, his partner drew a big, red heart in the middle of his brain. "Your intellect isn't your superpower, Timothy," she said. "Your heart is."

It was amazing to see his reaction. It looked like someone had pulled a plug from his back. His eyes grew huge and his jaw dropped. His shoulders relaxed, and he began to cry with a huge smile on his face. "Wow, wow, wow!" he replied.

"I've always felt something in me," he told us later on our podcast (see the Thank You page at the back of the book for a link to our podcast and more). "And hearing those words from my podmate made me realize that what I felt is light—my light.

When I'm at my best, I know that's what I'm tapping into. And I realized, what if I worked with it instead of hiding it?"

For Timothy, the larger light worked through a fellow human being, helping him see what he couldn't see on his own.

Intentionally Leading with the Larger Light

JEN'S STORY:

Tall pine, cedar, and birch trees surrounded me as I began my part in writing this book. I was at my 110-year-old family cabin in the woods of Rangely, Maine, settled in my grandmother's rocking chair, writing on the porch—or as they say in Maine, the "poch" (Mainers don't pronounce their r's). I asked the Universe, Spirit, and my angels and guides to work through me as a clear vessel to channel the light through my words. I also asked to be given blatantly obvious signs to help me stay connected to the muse and my diamond light.

My gaze alternated between the screen of my computer that laid on my lap and the serene lake just thirty yards beyond my feet. As I stared out into nature, I caught sight of a bald eagle soaring in the wind, only to land in the tree right in front of me. From studying the spiritual meaning of animals since I was a little girl, I knew this beautiful bird had a message for me. In some cultures, the eagle represents vision and the ability to see a higher perspective. For Americans, the eagle symbolizes freedom.

It was the perfect sign to encourage me to speak my truth as I embarked on the writing process.

And the signs kept coming, especially when I needed a nudge to keep going. When I returned home to Park City, my writing routine took place out on my back porch, early in the morning. One day, when I felt stuck, I noticed a wisp—a seed from one of the cottonwood trees in bloom. If you've ever seen the movie Avatar, *the wisps look very much like the white fairies that guide Jake Sully and Neytiri to their destination.*

The first time I noticed the wisp, I smiled. The second time I noticed the wisp in a different place and on a different day, I relaxed. The third time I noticed the wisp was inside the house—and then on the couch, and then in my car—I began to laugh. I see! I get it! Keep going!

And then, I noticed a pattern—the days where it felt hard to write and I had to force myself to push through, I wouldn't see the wisps. Yet, on the days when I felt open and in the flow, I would—and they would catch my attention in the most random places.

The wisps acted like signs from my spirit guides, nudging me along my path to continue writing. And that's how the larger light works. It works in the most mysterious ways to get our attention—that is, if we are paying attention.

Working with the larger light is on offer to all of us. In chapter 3, we introduced the river as a metaphor for conscious leadership.

We said the river flows on long before us and long after us, and where it flows, it goes. What if the river itself was the larger light? What if it knew exactly which way to take us? What would happen if we picked up our feet, leaned back, surrendered, and enjoyed the ride?

We can choose to either follow the current or exhaust ourselves trying to figure things out on our own, proving ourselves, pushing, pulling, and paddling upstream. The choice is always ours to make.

We believe the larger light has an intelligent benevolence. It is good. It has our backs. It wants the very best for us and from us. And when we stop struggling so much and let it lead us, we can often end up much further along than we imagined.

This may sound like it isn't for you, and that's okay. But for us, working with the larger light has helped us let go, release our grip, and surrender the need to figure everything out ourselves. We've made "following flow" a core value of our business at Plenty. We use that mantra daily in our decision-making, sales process, hiring, managing, and co-leadership. We've learned to attune to the current of what is working, rather than what is not.

It's not a game-changer for us. It's a life-changer.

Following flow requires us to surrender the belief that we dictate the current—surrender control, surrender the way, and surrender what we think the plan should be. It's the opposite of what we've been taught. Do we have a role? Yes—we each have a paddle, and our role is to steer along with it. But the river goes where the river flows.

When we say "following flow," we mean acknowledging that you don't and can't control everything. We mean looking for the current and momentum of energy. We mean dropping the desire or need to control every variable and person in your life. We mean meeting circumstances on their own terms instead of trying to twist them to how you wish them to be.

We've witnessed time and time again that if we rest our faith in the larger light to bring us the people, conversations, insights, and solutions we need, rather than pushing to find them ourselves, they come on their own, exactly when we need them to. When they come, they are more perfectly aligned, more perfectly timed, and more fitting than we could have imagined ourselves.

In other words, if something is upriver of you, it is easier to patiently wait for the current to bring it drifting right in front of you than it is to try to turn your canoe and paddle upstream.

Instead of choosing to control, you can choose to open, follow, and align with the larger light so you can co-create with it. "Co-creation" means a collaborative process to share wisdom and bring forth something new that will be for the greatest good of all involved. You can co-create with another person—as we did in cowriting this book—but you can also co-create with the light around you.

This intention requires practice and experimentation and a shift from head to heart. It's a nonlinear, intuitive practice that calls forth a new level of partnership. For us, co-creating with the larger light has led us to trust what we can't always prove, explain, or understand. It helps us move forward in faith when thing don't go our way—a sales deal falls through, a client needs to shift the dates of a retreat, and so forth. Trusting the larger light—following the flow of the river—has led us to experience more happiness, abundance, and fulfillment in leading ourselves and others than we could have ever imagined.

This invitation is on offer for you too.

Co-Creating with Light

Ever try to learn to play golf? Or if you play regularly, do you remember when you first learned?

It looks pretty simple from afar. You stand at the first green and watch the foursome ahead of you haul off on some beautiful drives. You watch what they are doing, and it doesn't look too complex. You get to stand right over the ball, and the ball doesn't even move!

When it is your turn, you take a tight hold of the driver, twist your back and bend your arms, and put everything you have into the swing. Thwack. The ball moves about four feet sideways. Hmmm. Maybe you could use a lesson.

When you head to the driving range, you're surprised that the very first thing the pro tells you is *relax your grip*. It doesn't sound right, but the pro coaches you to hold the club so loosely you think it is going to fly out of your hand. And it helps. A lot. Turns out the club can't do its work with you gripping it like a vise.

It's amazing how much good advice starts with loosening rather than tensing. It's not just athletic advice, either. You can type faster if you don't try to destroy the keys. You play the piano better if you think of dropping from the elbow rather than pounding with your hands. You can sing higher notes by learning how to relax your throat with each subsequent pitch.

And yet, a lot of modern self-leadership is about checklists, operational plans, daily meetings, and regular routines. We learn to tighten our hold on ourselves (and others) instead of loosening up. Where's the room to let life do its work?

Accepting the idea that you can't—and don't—engineer everything in your life opens up a bit of space to let the light in. Whether you choose to see that as divine timing or random chance is a matter of choice. But the Universe works in part through unanticipated interventions—from an asteroid strike bringing new elements to a planet, to birds bringing new seeds to a garden.

If your workday is scheduled from 8:00 a.m. to 6:00 p.m., where is the time to bump into the new business association in the lobby? Or engage in the daydreaming that leads to a new solution?

If your social life is tightly choreographed, where is the opportunity to encounter the person who might become your new best friend?

If your emotional life is controlled to protect you from all stress, fear, and opinions that you disagree with, where will you find the spark of something new?

It sounds counterintuitive, but conscious leadership means trusting that you can loosen your grip. You don't have to do it all alone. You can't do it all. You can ask the world around you to help you and trust the help you receive—even when it doesn't come in the form you expected.

Co-Leading with Light

We experience a range of emotions from our participants when we talk about the Fourth Light: There Is a Larger Light Guiding Us. Some look visibly relieved to receive confirmation that they don't have to figure it all out! Some are moved to hear validation of something they've known to be true in their lives. And some seem a bit shaken, almost uncertain.

"I know what you mean about loosening up," we'll hear. "I can be wound pretty tight. But that's what got me to where I am now. I've become successful because of all my hard work. And now you're telling me to stop?"

We've learned to wink and respond with a profound question: How do you know your hard work is what has gotten you to this point?

When you're learning a skill, there's no doubt of the power of repetition. If you practice correctly, your golf swing will improve as you go to the driving range. You will become a better lacrosse player or hockey player the more you pick up your stick. You will be able to increase your deadlifts or bench presses if you do them every week. You will get better at piano if you practice every day.

But life is more than a skill. There's a massive amount to it that has nothing whatsoever to do with you. Whether you view it as fate, chance, luck, or destiny, often the things that are most impactful in our lives are the things we never anticipated or had any real part in choosing. We steer with our paddle, yes, but we don't change the current.

As we become more aware and aligned to the creative, divine intelligence running through us all the time, we can learn to let go and allow life to take us where it wants to go. When we allow the larger light to work its magic, we can begin to see evidence of its power and grace, its capacity to know exactly what we need at exactly the right time. When we start to trust that it knows what we need when we need it, we don't have to work so hard to get what we think we want.

When you begin to really experience that you are living in this current, you begin to ride the wave of being human with more joy and ease. You start to trust more deeply that when you need an answer to a challenge or problem, the solution will always come at the perfect time (which may not always be when you want it to). You begin to witness the magic in the muse bringing forth the exact insight, person, or solution you need at just the right time. You see that you really couldn't have orchestrated or planned what unfolded, and as you notice that orchestration, you stand in awe. You take note of the intelligence of the light that is within and the light that comes with you wherever you go.

At Plenty, we have done our best to co-lead with light in everything we do. We've practiced acknowledging that we don't do it all on our own and can't control it all. Whether it be preparing sacred space for executives and clients who come into HeartSpace, showing up at a meeting, or walking in the door at home after a long workday, we invite light in. We ask the light to use us for the highest and greatest good of all. We ask for help in bringing harmony, healing, and abundance into the moment—or whatever our intention is for the work at hand. We practice presence and trust in when we need to lead, weave, or listen. It hasn't been easy, but it has gotten a lot more playful. The more we've practiced, the more comfortable, confident, and clear we've become.

When we co-lead with light, we do our part and surrender the rest. We allow the higher light to work through us. It unites with our individual lights so we can become vehicles for the larger light to do its work. That's how we can bring the formless into form.

Co-leading with light is an invitation on offer for you and all conscious leaders. It may look and feel different to you, and it likely works in different ways for you than it does for us. But when you begin to open yourself to something greater than your own will and ego, you can begin to see evidence of the muse all around. And when you notice these signs and synchro-nicities, you can choose to ignore them and brush them off as happenstance, or you can get curious as to what they point to and what they mean. It may take a bit of inquiry, but if you choose to go beyond, the answers surface and you discover what the higher light wants you to see. And you may just find that you light yourself up in the process.

What will spring forth when you ask to be an open channel to uplift the world?

Each one of us is being called to listen, to weave, and to co-create with the larger light guiding us in the way that works best for us. We are asked to bring all that we are and all that wants to express itself through us is into our workplace, our home, and wherever we choose to show up.

Co-leading with light shows us the evidence we don't have to lead alone. We always have a partner who wants to play. That partner is a higher intelligence showing us where the current is. It's leaving us clues all the time. It's pointing us to where the flow is. Do you see it?

PRACTICE POINTS

PRACTICING THE FOURTH LIGHT

There Is a Larger Light Guiding Us

Notice the Higher Light

What would it feel like to completely trust and believe that a larger light is guiding you and supporting every step you take? Notice the signs and synchronicities that capture your attention, and instead of writing them off as "weird coincidences" or random happenstance, try on the notion that each has been placed on your path for an important reason. Witness the perfection and personalization of this force—giving you the answers you need, placing people on your path, and dropping clues to inform your next step. Follow them and celebrate where they take you.

At the end of your day, make note of the magic, the signs, and the synchronicities that crossed your path.

- Who did you feel connected to?

- Where did you feel most enlivened?

- Where was the beauty in your day?

Ask for Help

Call in your angels, spirits, guides, God, the Universe, or Spirit (whatever you name them to be). Ask them to be a part of your day, to be with you as you walk, to co-create with you, or to show you signs of their existence. Don't wait to be on the basement floor or hit by a Mack Truck. Rather, start your day with intentional communion with the larger light guiding you. Here are a few statements you may wish to try:

- Great Spirit, use me in the highest service of the light today.

- Angels and guides, please help me receive, bring, and be the light everywhere I go.

- Dear Universe, help me see the signs and synchronicities that abound, so I may know exactly what to do and where to be in order to serve my highest good and the highest good of all.

- God, show me a clear sign today that I am where I need to be.

Trust the Signs

Everywhere we turn, there are cues and clues appearing in our field to help guide our next step. The question is, are we noticing them?

Signs can come in many different forms. They may emerge in patterns from seemingly disconnected sources, like when three different people mention the same book to read or suggest the same place to visit. Or signs may come in the form of numbers, like 11:11 or 4:44, that you notice throughout the day. Or they may come in the form of an animal that crosses your path, or when different team members all speak to something that needs to be improved in your business at different times and in different ways.

If everything is connected, then everything has a purpose and a place. Sometimes, discovering the meaning behind the sign takes a bit of inquiry.

To discover the meaning behind numbers, download the 11:11 Oracle App by Alana Fairchild. When you see a number pattern that catches your attention, simply enter it in and read the meaning. Or, search for the "spiritual meaning of 11:11." Allow yourself to receive the guidance that is on offer for you.

To understand the meaning of an animal that flies or walks into your view, look it up! Get out your phone and do a quick search for "the spiritual meaning of [the animal's name]." Notice what message the animal has for you. Does it provide inspiration in the moment? Does its spirit help show you what next step to take?

Pay attention to the signs.

Fuel Faith, Not Fear

We live in a world that wants to limit us. But our light has no limit. You're never given a problem that doesn't have some sort of solution. One of Thich Nhat Hanh's lovely quotes points to this: "Because you're alive, everything is possible." And, as

Jennifer's grandmother loved to say, "Where there's a will, there's a way!"

When fear overcomes you, it's helpful to remember what we related back in chapter 4: that FEAR can also be thought of as an acronym for "False Evidence Appearing Real," as coined by author Neale Donald Walsch. He's pointing to the idea that what we fear is often made up in our minds. It may look real, but more often than not, the evidence of it is an illusion. Remembering this shift in perspective can help short-circuit the train of thought and neuropathway that wants to buy the fearful thinking, which only leads to ideations and projections of worst-case scenarios.

The antidote to fear is FAITH—an acronym for "Fully Anticipating It To Happen." We get to choose what the "it" is, as we place our focus and attention on that which we want to manifest. Do we want to manifest incredible things to happen? Or more things to be fearful about?

We all have a choice as to which thought (and hence feeling) we want to feed. Make conscious choices about the reality that you want to manifest, and create your own momentum.

Pick a Card

Oracle decks, tarot cards, and wisdom cards have been around for centuries. They've been used as tools to help human beings find their way. For us, we've used them for decades to help guide our day, connect to the light within, and stay aligned to our united lights as we lead our clients and company. There are many to choose from, but our very favorite creators are Alana Fairchild, Denise Linn, Alberto Villoldo, and Jamie Sams.

A quick search on Amazon or Google for "spirit card decks," "oracle card decks," "animal wisdom card decks," "sacred geometry card decks," or "tarot card decks" will surface hundreds of options. Choose one that speaks to you.

Once your card deck has arrived, take out all the cards and clear them. You can do this by knocking your fist on the deck three times, blowing on it with your breath, cleansing it with burning sage smoke, or placing it on your heart.

As you do one of these actions, set your intention for the deck to align with the energy and purpose of your heart. You can silently say to yourself, "May these cards resonate with the passions and purpose of my heart as they guide me to my highest and greatest good." Use whatever intention feels good to you; just ask the cards to help you align to your own light.

Then, shuffle the cards and pick the first card that captures your attention. Once you do, read about the wisdom of the card and notice what you notice. You can also do a three-card spread or follow the specific directions from the creator that come with each deck. We know you will be blown away by the wisdom your light holds for you.

Meditate

Meditation is an accessible way to calm your inner landscape. Now, meditation may be old hat for some, while for others it may be intimidating. But you already have done it, no matter whether you view the practice to be easy or hard. You've been in a meditative state when you sleep. You've been in a meditative state when you are quiet in nature. You've been in a meditative state when you are creating something of beauty and lose track of time. Meditation creates spaciousness between our thoughts.

Meditation can happen on a walk in nature, or while running, painting, or making music. It doesn't have to look a certain way. It works best for the two of us sitting or lying down, listening to peaceful music, and closing our eyes to tune in. Find whatever way works for you and make time for it. Bring it into your work life. Start a meeting with it. Take a break with it. Start or end your day by being still. Doing so can help you tap into the greater force that wants to flow through you, and you just might be pleasantly surprised at what is illuminated for you.

Make time to slow down and tune in. Practice being present and quieting your monkey mind, the critical inner voice that can hijack your thinking. Look for the light that exists within you for the answers. Invite the higher light to infuse you.

See the Thank You page at the end of the book for more information about our channeled and guided meditations.

Be the Tool

There's no better tool than you—and yes, we get the pun. What we mean is you have everything you need within you. Your light comes with you wherever you go, and it is connected to the infinite well of the Universe.

You are the tool! Although we've shared a lot of tools to help you practice conscious leadership, nothing compares to the wisdom of your light. Trust it. Listen to your intuition and intellect, and lead with your heart. Trust that you are equipped and ready for every moment that greets you, even if you doubt it. Trust you will know what to say and what to do in every single moment if you tune in to listen. Trust that you are ready, right this very moment, to greet life with your whole, open heart.

Life needs you. The world needs you. The light needs you to shine!

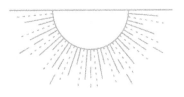

CHAPTER 8

Choosing Abundance

What's with Everyone Today?

Have you ever had one of those days where *you're* being totally perfect but everyone else just seems to be a total asshole?

Your partner didn't pick up their laundry, again, and when you asked nicely, they totally snapped at you. The barista at Starbucks got your order wrong, and when you politely pointed it out, everyone else in line glared at you. When you got to work, your team had the meeting time wrong (though you forgot to send out the calendar invite), and so everyone else was late except you. You phone your mom, and gawd she's so touchy!

"Wow," you think to yourself. "What is *with* everyone today?!"

You're perplexed all day until you get home after work. Your partner kindly says, "Are you okay? You seemed a bit on edge this morning."

And then it hits you: Oh, shoot. Everyone else was fine. *I'm the asshole.*

Ah, the power of awareness!

Finding Yourself Again

As you begin to use the Four Lights of Conscious Leadership to help you practice being more aware, aligned, and intentional, you may start to notice some surprising benefits. You may feel like you aren't triggered as much. You may feel like you spend fewer days wondering what is *wrong* with everyone else and a few more days being grateful for who *you* are.

You may feel like life is, well, a little slower. That you don't get as revved up as often as you used to—that you are able to laugh at yourself a bit more.

You may notice you don't get as anxious, and that when you do, you're able to shift your feelings with thoughts of gratitude.

You may feel a bit removed from your problems and challenges—and when something unexpected pops up in your path, you don't immediately sabotage your entire day reacting to it.

On that note, you may feel less reactive in general. You may feel like you are leading your life instead of being dragged along behind it.

You may notice more beauty in your conversations, creations, and day.

You may feel more present, less distracted, and less stressed.

Very simply, you may feel happier.

The Most Important Conversation

We first met Tamara at Lantern, our leadership retreat, about five years ago. Like most of our attendees, she was accomplished and talented. A scientist and manager, Tamara was used to being excellent at everything she chose to do. But she had started to feel a bit lost—an uncomfortable feeling for someone accustomed to being the most competent person in the room.

She came into the week thoughtful but reserved, with the polished presence of someone used to putting forth a carefully crafted version of herself.

Over the next day, we watched as Tamara slowly emerged from her self-imposed shell. One of the magical things about Lantern is that the real work happens in small group conversations. We noticed that as Tamara listened to others sharing, she become more willing to share herself.

And amid those small group conversations, there's another more important conversation: the conversation each person is having with *themselves*. It's the conversation that is ongoing in all our minds, all the time. It's the conversation you're having right now, even as you read this book.

It's the conversation in which we tell ourselves we were born for this—or that we're just another failure. It's the one where we say that this is interesting—or a waste of time. It's the one where we decide to craft a choreographed, manicured version of ourselves to share—or say, "Screw it, it's too hard to hide who I am anymore."

As we watched Tamara, we could tell there were some big discussions going on inside her head and heart. It was if she was starting to go deep in dialogue with herself. She was slowing down in her speech, writing in her journal more. She was tearing up from time to time.

It looked like she was getting honest with herself.

Toward Your Light

As our attendees share the retreat experience, their group discussions become more deeper and more vulnerable—not because we've "pushed people out of their comfort zone" (a phrase we truly despise), but because the zone of what is comfortable has *expanded*, simply through growing honesty and trust.

Over the week, we watched as Tamara slowly opened up. It was messy at first. And that's okay—we're all messy in places. She cried a lot, sometimes without even knowing *what* she was crying about! When we had our closing circle on Friday afternoon, Tamara shared with the group that she felt on the edge of something new and better.

"It's like coming back home to myself," she said. "It's like meeting my true self again."

We kept in touch with her, on and off, and were pleased to see her name show up on the registration list for Lumeria, our wellbeing retreat, in the spring.

When we met her at the door of HeartSpace, we couldn't believe she was the same person. We couldn't believe the difference in just six months. She looked the same—but there was something more there. A spark, an energy. Her face had a permanent smile but also a deep calmness. She appeared more relaxed and secure in herself. She focused on each of us fully as she talked, keeping eye contact. She listened to our responses without interrupting and sometimes responded only with a smile.

We knew what was different. It was light. Her light.

"Wow, Tamara! You look incredible!" we said.

"I feel incredible," she replied. "I can't tell you how much I've grown. I stopped trying so much. I stopped pushing so hard. And in the open space, I found my soul."

Worry Doesn't Work

Time and again, we've heard stories like this from the people with whom we work. Some of the transformations, like Tamara's, are stunning. New jobs, new relationships, new careers, new trajectories.

Others are more subtle but equally groundbreaking. Less stressed. Less anxious. More present. More confident. A feeling of renewed faith.

What happens?

Do our attendees have fewer problems after Lantern than they did before? We don't think so. In fact, participants often stay in touch with us and report on the difficulties they encounter as they continue to travel down the river. What we love is that many attendees leave Lantern and step more fully out into the world, embracing new careers, relationships, and paths that end up putting *more* challenges in their way.

No, the change isn't in the ease of our attendees' lives. The change is in the ease of their *hearts*.

JEFF'S STORY:

About ten years ago, Jen and I were building the basics of Plenty. It was an exciting time and a tumultuous one. We were changing the focus of the company, the team, the kind of clients we took—almost everything about the firm. There was a ton of stress involved.

As we held the first few sessions of Lantern, I realized I was the audience for many of the principles we were teaching! Here I was pointing people to a deeper, softer way of leading, and meanwhile, I was still trying to press, force, and push change as I helped manage Plenty. I started to see how often I was lost in future and past thinking—stressed about scenarios that hadn't happened yet, or worse, revving myself up by replaying situations in my head!

During the winter holiday break, my family and I were talking about New Year's resolutions, and I heard myself say, without really thinking about it, "I resolve to give up worry." Everyone laughed—it seemed like a frivolous comment, not to mention an elusive goal! But I was struck by the profound nature of the idea, almost as if someone else had said it.

Over the next few months, I intentionally practiced giving up the conceit of worry. I posted a banner on my Facebook page: "Worry doesn't work." It became my mantra. I got good at noticing how I used worry as a form of control, a way to grind my mind on things that I couldn't influence. I became present to my own use of the emotion in the same way someone living alcohol-free suddenly notices how much drinking exists in their friend group, or how someone trying to eat more healthily suddenly notices sugar on every ingredient label.

It was an amazing exercise for me. It was transformative. I won't say I live a life without worry. But the practice of setting the intention of how I wanted to be, and then noticing when I was on or off alignment, it dramatically improved my quality of life.

Putting Problems in Their Place

When you are living aligned to your energetic blueprint—confident in your own light, sure that it is on no matter how you feel, focused on the next step in front of you, and resting in the faith that you belong to this world—it's hard to take your problems as seriously as you did before. It's not to say that the problems aren't serious. It's to say that how we relate to them changes.

What if challenges are mandatory, but fear is optional? What if problems are part of life, but stress about them is simply a choice? What if we are meant to live the full spectrum of emotions to show us that we are alive and human?

What we notice in our clients and in ourselves is a certain kind of quiet knowing. It's a feeling that the challenges are here to help us be our best selves. It's an understanding that the challenges we face, the obstacles in our path, the accomplishments we make, are all interrelated. They are part of us. They are escorts to our becoming and agents for our growth. We don't have to be afraid of them or stressed by them.

In fact, how we choose to relate to ourselves—our challenges, strengths, weaknesses, and accomplishments—is the most fundamental freedom we have.

JEN'S STORY:

During the out-of-body experience I shared in chapter 4, I left out a significant part of my journey, as I didn't want you to lose the point I was trying to make. And honestly, it still feels vulnerable to write about it.

When I was being bathed in the unconditional light, out of my body, and generating ridiculous amounts of heat, a huge angelic being made itself known to me. It was a tall, iridescent figure standing at my feet. It must have been nine feet tall, glowing in yellow and blue light. Its presence was gentle yet strong and commanding. As I lay on the couch (out of my body in an altered state), this angelic being instructed me to heal the anterior cruciate ligament (ACL) in my knee. It asked me to direct my attention to it, and when I did, I could see exactly where the tear existed in my mind's eye.

The location of the injury was so specific that it was as if I had traveled inside the ligament itself. It glowed red/orange and I could see and feel the inflammation. The angelic being instructed me to blow cool air into it, and without thinking, I felt like I became superman, blowing cold, blue, icy air into the torn ligament. The area immediately calmed and changed color from red to blue, and in slow motion I could see every molecule and cell line up and repair itself. The ligament repaired itself in perfect alignment as if nothing had ever happened to it. I thanked the being for guiding me and I just knew the ACL was suddenly healed. Miraculously it was.

For the first time in four incidents of tearing my ACLs over my athletic career, I didn't need surgery. I had experienced complete healing of the knee.

Almost twenty years later, Jeff and I were working with Elsie Spittle, one of our own coaches in British Columbia. For some reason, this life-changing story came up, and I found myself retelling it. Even though I was in one of the safest places I could have imagined, I still felt vulnerable sharing it. As I did, Elsie listened intently. Then, she was quiet in her Master Yoda kind of way.

After several minutes sitting in silence she said, "Jennifer, what if you are the angel?"

This concept had never occurred to me before. But her words landed on my heart with a huge drop-the-mic feeling. A feeling of landing. A feeling of truth. A feeling of coming home to myself. A feeling of being connected to my higher light.

I began to cry as my breath was taken away.

Could I be the angel I was looking for? It never really occurred to me. But from that moment on, I began to see how what I seek has always been within. I am the healer I've been looking for.

Stepping into awareness doesn't happen all at once. None of us get to magically leave behind stress or fear in one week. But what happens is that we get to crack open that door a bit. We start to see the difference between ourselves and our thoughts. We start to see the beauty of our own potential. We start to see that the reasons we keep ourselves from our dreams are usually rooted in fears designed to protect us.

And as more light comes in through the door, the door gradually opens, further and further. And the further the door cracks open, the easier it is to move, and the more light comes in.

Eventually, we're bathed in the pure light of ourselves.

From Scarcity to Abundance

What would happen if, every time you faced a challenge, you started with the idea of, "Well, I'm not where I want to be right now, but I have within me the tools I need to start to change"?

When we see that we get to choose whether we walk in faith or not, the implications are profound. It's like moving from a world of limitations to a world of possibility.

We have a name for that world: a world of plenty. Not "Plenty," like our company name, but rather the idea that our company is named for: the idea of abundance. Our deepest belief, so deep that we named our work after it, is that people aren't competing with each other—they are competing with the idea that there isn't enough to go around.

We're competing with a mindset of scarcity.

Most of the practices we've outlined over these past chapters are ultimately designed to help you live past a world of limitation and into a world—and a *worldview*—of abundance. It's no small feat, because many of us were brought up, whether we know it or not, in a world that teaches us an underlying viewpoint of scarcity.

When we're small children, we're taught to share, enjoy, sing, and dance. We read aloud in a group. We throw and kick balls as a group, counting how many times we can do it. We laugh, watch television together, and take naps together. On snack day, we each bring a snack for everyone else. On our birthday, we bring treats for the *other* people in class.

If you've ever watched a nursery school class in session, you can see the idea of abundant community in action. The amount of sharing and caring between the small children is touching.

But after only a few years, our competitive instincts take over, primarily because our competitive instincts are the ones that get nurtured the most by the world around us. "Sharing and caring" becomes a snide punch line, said with a sarcastic snort. We learn to compare and measure ourselves against one another. Instead of running for play and exercise, we are taught to race. We rank who is better at throwing and kicking. In school, we begin to get tested and graded against one another.

By our teenage years, most of us have thoroughly absorbed the idea that for one person to win, everyone else must lose. We take that idea with us into college, business, politics, even religion, where the message is—again and again—that there's a finite pie. We are told, over and over, that there isn't enough to go around. Grades are given on a curve—for every A, there are ten Bs. Raises are given to the few people who earn a promotion. Most of the literature on business strategy is about beating the competition rather than creating new market space. And now we have social algorithms that reinforce and expand on that concept, choosing a few pieces of content by a few creators to get attention at the expense of everything else.

Do you see scarcity in your own thinking?

On our way back to HeartSpace after a sunrise hike during Lantern II, our annual reunion for Lantern graduates held every September, we were walking on either side of Brad on the paved path. Brad was distraught and confused. He kept looking at his Apple watch and muttering.

"What's the matter?" we asked.

Brad was frustrated. He said, "I don't get it! I walk all the time. How is this my record walk? I mean, I've walked great distances at a much faster pace than what we just did. How could this be my best time?"

His mood began to shift from a place of peace, connection, and openness to restless disappointment with his own performance. After the third time of watching him look down at his watch, Jennifer looked. "Brad, your watch isn't saying you just completed a record walk. It's asking you if you want to *record* your walk!"

All he had been able to see was a limited view that he didn't measure up. Immediately, Brad laughed out loud.

Scarcity thinking shows up in most of the people we work with. It is the undercurrent of many of the stories we've shared in this book: Katie, who felt stretched thin financially; Tim, who was so busy trying to maximize time that he ran into glass walls; and

Brad, who misunderstood what "record walk" meant. Scarcity vies for room in our own thinking, too—for example, in how we both feared that no one would hire us if our marketing showed who we truly were.

The idea that there isn't enough becomes embedded into most of us at a personal level, so deeply that often we don't even realize it. Consider that one of the most common modern laments is to avoid "wasting time"—as if time is a limited resource meant to be deployed, instead of a precious resource that is meant to be *enjoyed.*

Worse, we're not only taught that there's not enough to go around. We're also taught that we, ourselves, are not enough.

If you've ever lived with a teenager, as both of us do in our families right now, you'll realize how pervasive these messages of inadequacy are. Eliminate your blackheads. Lift your eyebrows. Flatten your belly. Grow your triceps. Post your selfie (multiple times a day)—but make sure it looks spontaneous. Buy trendy clothes to show you are different—but not too different. Be kind—but not obsequious. Be outgoing—but mysterious. Be unique—in the same way as everyone else.

Again and again, we learn to mold ourselves, shape ourselves, and condition ourselves, because the way we are isn't good enough. We're bombarded with messages that show us that our worth comes from the validation of others—and that such validation is finite in supply.

It's scary and sad—and while it may be the norm, it shouldn't be normal.

Abundance is your birthright, and it is built on three core beliefs:

- There is enough to go around.

- You have enough.

- You are enough.

There Is Enough to Go Around

Did you know that until the early 1800s, aluminum was regarded as the most precious metal in the world? In their book *Abundance*, Peter Diamandis and Steven Kotler relate the story. Aluminum was light, strong, shiny, and resistant to corrosion—but also hard to find and even harder to extract. At the state dinners, Napoleon III, the emperor of France, served his most important guests on aluminum plates—while the less important guests had to settle for tableware made of solid gold![6]

But less than fifty years later, chemists found an easy way to extract aluminum. The price of the substance plummeted, so much so that we hardly think about serving ourselves drinks out of containers made of this abundant, recyclable metal. Abundant? Yes—aluminum is the third most abundant element on earth. We just had to find a way to unlock it.

This anecdote illustrates perfectly what we mean by "There is enough to go around." What if all the problems we regard as problems of scarcity were actually problems of access or distribution or both?

---

6 Peter Diamandis and Steven Kotler, *Abundance: The Future Is Better Than You Think* (New York: Free Press, 2012).

"There's not enough fresh water." Really? Over 70 percent of the earth is water.[7] The problem is innovating the technology to desalinate the water we have and distribute it to those who need it.

"There is not enough food to feed all the hungry people." Really? The World Food Program estimates that nearly *one-third* of all food produced on the earth is lost, wasted, or thrown away before it can be consumed.[8] There is more than enough food to feed everyone person on the planet if we harness all of it.

"There's not enough clean energy." Renewables like wind and solar can provide vast amounts of clean, cheap energy, provided we make the investments to harness them.[9]

There isn't enough room for everyone. There isn't enough insight into the problem. There isn't enough time in the day. There isn't enough compassion in the world.

In his expansive 2018 book *Enlightenment Now*, social scientist Stephen Pinker makes a compelling case that is unpopular in our gloomy, stressed-out world: on literally every metric that measures human safety, satisfaction, and support, the world is demonstrably better off than it was one hundred years ago.[10] That doesn't mean there aren't problems. But we live in far more

---

7 Matt Williams, "What Percent of Earth Is Water?" Phys.org, December 2, 2014, https://phys.org/news/2014-12-percent-earth.html.

8 "5 Facts about Food Waste and Hunger," World Food Programme, June 2, 2020, https://www.wfp.org/stories/5-facts-about-food-waste-and-hunger.

9 "Renewable Energy – Powering a Safer Future," United Nations: Climate Action, n.d., https://www.un.org/en/climatechange/raising-ambition/renewable-energy. Accessed November 2, 2023.

10 Steven Pinker, *Enlightenment Now: The Case for Reason, Science, Humanism, and Progress* (New York: Viking Penguin, 2018).

prosperity than we notice—we have become inured to the miracles all around us. What if every dynamic of scarcity we can imagine could be reframed as a problem of access and distribution. How can we unlock that potential all around? How can we distribute in a way that fulfills that potential?

Moving from the macro to the micro: Do you see problems of scarcity in your own life? How could you reframe them?

What would *you* do if there were enough?

You Have Enough

When you genuinely believe there is enough to go around, you start to see the abundance you already have in your life right now. You start to see the difference between your wants and your true needs. And when you do find yourself in a place of true need, you realize that building on what you have, rather than lamenting what you don't, can be a massive advantage.

When we talk about the idea that "You have enough," we often get very emotional responses. People want to share their experiences, past and present, and want to talk about the dynamics of identity, privilege, prejudice, and discrimination. One powerful conversation played out as we were recording our podcast, *Plenty for Everyone.*

"It is one thing for white, educated people of privilege like the two of you to say, 'You have enough,'" one of our passionate friends and podcast guests said. "It is something very different for someone who is living outside in the slums of Chicago, the product of broken homes, drugs, and abuse, to see that what you're saying has any truth to it."

It's a powerful point. In no way are we trying to say the riches and abundance of the world are equitably *distributed*. As we wrote above, our worldview of abundance is built on the notion that there's enough to go around—not on the belief that it is always distributed fairly. We believe that one role of the conscious leader is to help unlock that abundance all around, for oneself and for others. We believe a world of plenty for everyone is possible with conscious application and intent.

When we write "You have enough," we're not talking necessarily about material possessions, access to resources, or even peace of mind. We are describing an orientation, a way of thinking.

We mean, start with the idea that you already have everything you need to begin.

That doesn't mean you have to do it alone. Society has a role, government has a role, business has a role, and family has a role. What it means, though, is that we start with ourselves. *We start where we are.*

Have you—or your kids—ever watched one of those videos on YouTube where someone challenges themselves to see if they can trade a penny for a house? There are hundreds of varieties of this now. It's amazing. The host will take a small object—a penny, a pen, a piece of gum—and over the course of a few weeks, trade it, slowly at first, for bigger and bigger objects, until a month later, they are living in their own house.

It's somewhat fanciful and contrived, but it speaks to the essence of what we're trying to get at. One of Plenty's earliest taglines was "More from many." A worldview of abundance is built on two interdependent feelings: gratitude and generosity. There's gratitude for the gifts we have and a willingness to share them with others. Together doesn't mean less. Sharing doesn't mean finding yourself half full. The conscious leader understands that generosity encourages more giving and that giving generates receiving.

Stone Soup

A traveler comes into a town pub at night talking about the magical stone he'll use to make soup—the best soup anyone has ever tasted. The villagers gather around, curious and doubtful, as the stranger asks for a cauldron, fills it with water, and sets it next to the fire. Plop! He throws in the stone and waits.

"I can't wait to share this lovely soup with all of you," he says.

The villagers mumble with skepticism, but one says, "You know, I bet stone soup is better with potatoes." She runs home, grabs her sack of potatoes, and adds them to the pot.

"Well," says the innkeeper, "no soup is good without salt and pepper," and she sprinkles both in. Another nods as he adds carrots. "Carrots will taste good, too."

Soon others have joined in, and fresh chicken, barley, thyme, and parsley are added too.

It turns out the traveler was right: it was the best soup anyone had ever tasted.

When we say, "You have enough," we aren't telling you that you don't have to pay rent or that a wish will elevate you above food stamps, any more than we are saying that good intentions alone with help you find your spouse, your career, or your life's purpose.

What we're saying is, the choice starts with deciding what you want to make from the stone. Is it cold, hard, and useless? Or is it the beginning of the best meal you've ever tasted? (Incidentally, the story of stone soup is also a wonderful metaphor for mobilizing your community or your team. Everyone has a unique part to play, and every part matters.)

Whatever mindset you choose to take, and wherever you place your attention, you feed. What you feed forms. When you place your attention on all that you have to be grateful for, you usher in more to be grateful for. When you place your attention on wanting more, you perpetuate the distance between where you are right now and your wanting. Are you feeding more feelings of lack? Or are you feeding more feelings of abundance?

What would change if you felt like you had enough?

You Are Enough

And now we've arrived at the most fundamental point—the core essence of our work at Plenty, our mindset of abundance, and really, this very book.

What if you, right now, as you are, were enough?

Think of it.

What if you weren't broken or deficient? What if you didn't need to improve or change? What if you were more magnificent than you could imagine? What if you had everything inside of yourself to thrive?

What if you were enough, just as you are right now?

Maybe your problems and challenges aren't a sign of being held back, but a playground to show you how resilient and creative you are.

Maybe your fears and insecurities aren't indications that you are flawed, but reminders to trust in your uniqueness and have faith.

Maybe your individual talents and interests aren't peculiar, but are instead a specific ingredient needed to perfect the recipe of the world.

Maybe you were put here for a reason so special and so unique that you are the one single person who could fulfill it.

What if you didn't have to change anything to be more seen? Loved? Understood? Appreciated? Rewarded?

Yes, you live in a world of eight billion people, and that can make any of us feel lost, lonely, and unneeded at times—until you consider that there is literally not one single person exactly like you. Not one.

You are one in eight billion.

What if you stopped trying to be less different?

In fact, what if the one monumental challenge of this life is to learn to be more yourself?

PRACTICE POINTS

PRACTICING ABUNDANCE

Become Aware of
Your Abundant Mindset

What would change about your outlook if you oriented yourself toward abundance instead of scarcity? What does a world of abundance mean to you?

Notice Your Language

- Do you catch yourself saying, "There just isn't enough . . ." when you talk about money, time, resources, and opportunities? What changes if you say, "I have everything I need." What shifts?

- Pay attention to the number of times you criticize, berate, and talk down to yourself. "I look so tired this morning. I'm so overweight. These jeans don't fit. My eyes are so baggy." What happens if you choose a different way? "I'm right where I need to be. I'm fine exactly how I am. I am living my life right now, and I grow every day."

Align with Abundance

What would happen if you realigned your thinking to a mindset of abundance?

- Can you practice saying, simply, "There's enough to go around" the next time you find yourself in a mood of scarcity, jealousy, or envy?

- How can you align the messages you take in with the worldview you want to share? Note that this doesn't mean cutting yourself off from the world or celebrating ignorance. But it does mean aligning your routines so that you don't wake up reacting to whatever is playing out in the latest news cycle. How can you find messages that are positive and reinforcing? How can you seek out news that feels good to you?

Choose Abundance

Practice entering each day and situation with gratitude for what you have been given and the intention to share it rather than hoard it. "Today I will share my gifts in service of the group."

- What shifts in you as you contemplate sharing what you have instead of accumulating more? Do you notice how those gifts come back to you?

- When you find you are stuck in a place of scarcity, how can you spend intentional time sharing and giving away? Donating time, talent, and treasure is a powerful way to reconnect with the gifts we carry and create all around.

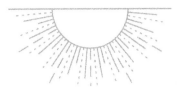

CHAPTER 9

Tapping Yourself

We used to close our Lantern retreat with a short exercise that we picked up three decades ago, when we were facilitating leadership development sessions for college students. We're not sure who created it or the original source, but we call it the Leadership Tap.

You can try it yourself.

Get comfortable in your chair. Put both feet on the ground, and sit up straight (but comfortably). Let yourself relax. Notice if there's rigidity in your body anywhere. Notice the sounds around you, and let any distractions be okay. Notice your mind—is it busy? Are you thinking about other things, or are you present here? Do your best to bring your attention back here, to the words on the page.

You may wish to close your eyes to settle further.

Now, when you feel a tap on the head, you may open your eyes, stand up, and move around.

Don't get up until you feel the tap.

Did you feel it?

When we would facilitate the exercise during Lantern, we'd have dozens of people sitting with their eyes closed in our main retreat room at HeartSpace. We'd have to repeat the sentence over and over: "When you feel a tap on the head, you may open your eyes, stand up, and move around." Often, the groups might sit for five or six minutes.

Eventually, someone realizes the point: Oh, no one is going to tap me.

I have to tap myself.

Waiting for the Sign

As it turns out, after our first ten or so sessions of our leadership retreat, Lantern, we stopped using the Leadership Tap, at least in the way we've outlined it here. There's probably no single activity that created more discussion—and at times, more negative feedback.

Many of our participants found the activity thought provoking. "Wow, I would have sat there all day. What a metaphor."

But one or two of our participants at every session would leave troubled. Some participants felt like we were pulling a fast one on them. "After a week of safe conversation, I felt manipulated" was a common piece of feedback. "I knew you were trying to get me to realize something, but I didn't want to have to guess" was another.

We have exactly zero room for—or interest in—manipulation in our work, so we listened to the feedback of those participants and have adapted the exercise to be fully supportive rather than potentially experienced as manipulative. (You'll have to come to Lantern yourself to see how.)

But we believe deeply in the intent behind the exercise. The amount of feedback the exercise generates shows us that the substance of the Leadership Tap pulls deeply at the soul.

What if the Universe is tapping us all the time, nudging us to become what we're most meant to become? What if we've learned to dismiss those taps as silly dreams, impractical ideas, or unrealistic projects not worth pursuing?

What if the sign we're ready for something more is when we first ask ourselves, "Am I really ready?"

Praying for the Fire

Often, we work with leaders who are waiting for *The Sign*.

"I have a feeling this business unit isn't going to perform any longer. How do I know for sure?"

"I'm not sure my boyfriend is the right fit for me, and I don't think he ever was. How can I be certain?"

"The person I hired to be my new vice president feels a bit off to me. What would you recommend I do to assess them?"

"I'm realizing that I don't always like what I'm doing anymore. But everyone feels that way, right?"

Can you give me the sign?

We sometimes hear a more dramatic version of this kind of looking for the sign. We'll never forget years ago when we met

Joseph. An energetic entrepreneur, Joseph has a way of lighting up every room he's in. Joseph embodies the idea that there aren't any strangers—only friends you haven't met yet.

When Joseph came into our retreat, it might have been the loudest first evening we've ever held. He had his small group in stitches all evening, so much so that people in the other pods were kind of staring at the group that was swept up in hysterical laughter, wondering what they were missing out on.

As often happens at Lantern, those first impressions gave way to a more nuanced, three-dimensional impression by the second day. Joseph was deep in stress and worry. His business, which looked successful on the outside, was hemorrhaging money. He was running out of credit to keep it functioning. Even worse, it was demanding every waking moment of his day. Normally active and healthy, he was starting to gain weight, lose sleep, and experience pains in his chest and thighs.

His group challenged him a bit. You still have assets—can't you sell the business? You're young and talented; why not go work for someone else for a while?

Joseph was adamant that he wouldn't quit. "No, no, I can't bail out now. But I often find myself wishing . . . oh, I don't know . . . what would be so great is if a huge fire burned my warehouse to the ground. I'd get insurance money and I'd be free to do something else. Honestly, I find myself fantasizing about that."

We were really struck by this vulnerable confession. Can you imagine feeling so out of options and so helpless that you literally hope a major catastrophe will force your hand?

Awareness Is the Tap

The more we work with high-performing leaders, the more we hear expressions exactly like Joseph's.

"I just wish someone would buy us."

"I wish the board would finally fire me."

"I wish an earthquake would turn it all to rubble."

The comments are similar to what we hear from people struggling with their relationships. "Sometimes I just wish he would have an affair and leave me" we'll hear. If clients are struggling with alcohol, we might hear, "Sometimes I pray I'll get in a car wreck—not that I want to hurt anyone, but because then I'd know I actually needed to go to rehab."

We've learned that it is quite common for successful people to lock up when they encounter uncertainty about their purpose. After years of tackling every challenge in their path, they find themselves disoriented when they aren't sure where to go next. The uncertainty is new. The feeling of paralysis is uncomfortable. It is easier to ask for intervention from the outside than it is to figure out how to get back on track.

It's probably not surprising when you think of it. People who have enjoyed a certain amount of accomplishment aren't always that practiced in getting *stuck* in hard situations. They have practice in *overcoming* obstacles—*which is different from practice in being stopped by them.*

But just as boulders in the river curve the flow of the water, obstacles in our own lives challenge us to change our path. The question is, how many times do you want to run into the rocks before you do?

We've come to believe that awareness *is* the sign. When you look ahead and see a massive rock in the river, that's the nudge you need to move your paddle and change course. You wouldn't let yourself run into the rock first and then ask, "Can I get a sign if I should steer around this?"

In other words, when you first become aware that the business isn't performing, your boyfriend might not be right for you, your new employee isn't working out, or your career isn't fulfilling—well, that's the sign you were looking for. Your moment of awareness is the sign.

But once you have awareness of your true desires and dreams, the Universe has done its part of the job. It's now on you to decide what to do about it.

You've got to be the one to tap yourself on the head, stand up, and move around.

The Joy of Moving Forward

Do you remember when you first learned to ride a bike? It looked like freedom and fun. It also looked scary and unpredictable. The seat seemed so high off the ground. The pedals were a bit of a stretch for your legs, and the handlebars had a way of twisting when you didn't want them to. And most dangerously, to get your feet in the right place, you had to take them off the ground! Every time you tried to get on, the bike would start to fall over.

Many of us had an older sibling or a parent or a friend who would hold the bike steady while we got everything in place. Yes, that feels better—everything is easier to balance when someone else is holding the bike.

But then you wonder, "Wait, how does this work exactly? I see all my friends riding around without their parents trailing behind them. How do I get started after I fall over if no one is holding onto me? The faster I go, the more I need someone to steady me, right?"

The miracle that you discover is that the opposite is true. *The faster you move, the easier it is to balance.* Rather than becoming more precarious as you pedal, the bike becomes *easier* to control as you pick up speed. Perhaps you've had the chance to appreciate that memory from the parent's perspective, too.

Even for people who have ridden a bike for thirty years, balancing a bike is hardest when it isn't moving. That's also the point at which it is most difficult to pedal. There are too many forces to easily keep in equilibrium, and a lot of exertion is needed to move the pedals and get the wheels moving. But add a bit of forward momentum, even a slight push from your feet, and suddenly you're on your way.

Getting Moving

In the process of writing this book, we learned to trust our own advice in a deeper way than we ever have before. The entire focus of the book changed as we talked—from an explanation of the seven points of our Lantern Leadership Model to a simpler but deeper exposition of the Four Lights you're holding now.

We hit snags we didn't know we'd hit as we tried to wrestle with some topics that didn't want to be wrestled and fit in other topics that didn't want to fit. We found ego struggles we thought we had already overcome, as our own territoriality about who would write which sections surfaced in surprising ways. We felt challenged writing asynchronously in different locations.

And in the process, we created *twenty-four* different versions of the outline before we even started writing. We probably would still be working on outlines if at one point our publishers Catherine and Nathan didn't politely say, "Now it's time. Just start writing."

We resisted and protested, we asked for delays, and we said we needed to be sure. They were polite but firm. "Start writing."

And so, we did. And as we got the pedals moving, the book started to pick up speed. We found clarity and a joy we couldn't get to in the outline stage. We just needed to take the next step. We needed to get moving.

In chapter 6, we talked about the Third Light of Conscious Leadership, the idea that you only have to see what is right in front of you. We hear time and time again how helpful and groundbreaking that piece of insight is. You don't have to figure it all out—and frankly, you *can't*. It's not just that you "only need" to see what is right in front of you. You only *can* see what's right in front of you.

Similarly, it can be tempting to pause and ask for advice. Surely others have been here, right? Surely someone can point you on your way.

There's no doubt that perspective is valuable. As coaches and consultants for others, we hire coaches and consultants ourselves to help us consider new ideas and point us to new experiences. But we still must do the learning ourselves. See, perspective is different from *instructions*. It's one thing to hear, "When I came to that boulder in the river, I tried to go wide right and stay in the shallows." It's another thing altogether to try to push the paddle against the current while the spray is hitting you smack in the face.

No one else can operate the machine that is you. There aren't any instructions for how to navigate the things that are standing in your way. That's *why* those things are holding you up in the first place—if you knew how to navigate them, they wouldn't have stopped you, right?

Yes, planning is important. Advice is important. But when you finally have that moment of awareness—or the awareness that you've had *many* moments of awareness, over and over—usually the best thing to do is to take one next step. That doesn't mean "take all the steps." You don't have to ride to the next town. But it helps to set the analysis aside, get your butt in the seat, and start pedaling.

What is the next step you could take, right now?

A Strange Game

Imagine you are invited to participate in a great game. The field stretches wide and green under a bright blue sky. You see other participants around you, milling about on the field. Some are stretching out. Some are talking with one another. A few seem lost in deep contemplation, others in stress.

Everyone is wondering what type of game it will be. Competitive? Cooperative? Do we need to run or throw? Or perhaps it is a scavenger hunt or a word challenge?

Eventually, the organizer arrives, steps up on a ladder with a bullhorn, and announces the rules. It turns out to be a bit strange: You can pick any activity you want. You don't get to know how long the game lasts. But you do get to choose how you will *feel* when it ends.

Huh? What? The group of people looks around in confusion. Those are the only rules? The organizer will tell us when the time is up, we get to do whatever we want, and we can decide how we feel when it's over?

What would you choose to feel? Accomplished? Proud? Loved? Grateful? Or would you choose to feel confused, angry, alone, sad, and regretful?

What would you choose to do? Would you pick an activity that everyone else wanted you to do? Or would you do what you liked best?

And how would you choose to play? Would you hold back, not knowing when it was going to end, trying to conserve your energy? Or would you go all out with the understanding that it could end at any moment?

It's a strange game. And we're all playing it.

It's called life.

What do you want to do with yours?

Living into Your Legacy

What do you think of when you hear the word "legacy"? How do you think of your legacy?

From our experience, most people think of legacy in terms of what they want to leave *behind* for others. Memories, love, accomplishment, perhaps a house or an inheritance. In this sense, legacy means creating something that we can give away, or perhaps that others can be proud of. Legacies, though, are not always positive. We may leave our children with debt or emotional hardship or wrecked relationships.

Or, we might think of the legacy from the perspective of what we've inherited. Again, it could be money, an estate, debt, love, abuse, burdens, ease, obligation, or aspirations.

Legacy has a dual sense, then, of what we bring from the past and what we love into the future.

But what if we looked at legacy in a third way, from the perspective of the present?

At any one point, *your present legacy is the sum of your own investment in yourself*—how you're present with your past and your future, together.

We each receive a balance of positive and negative from and in our life. But like the lantern we hold above our heads to illuminate what is right in front of us, our legacy is always being conceived, written, and revised as we live. There's nothing that's set in stone while we're still incarnated on the earth.

The Questions of Legacy

Bringing your legacy into the present means thinking about the positives and negatives you've inherited—and the ones you're creating to leave behind—and, as always, making conscious choices about what you see and sense.

What feels fresh now? Where do you light up and lean in? Where do you find yourself delaying, avoiding, or procrastinating?

Are you accomplishing what you want to? Or are you leaving some of your potential untapped? Are you playing all out, or do you have more to give to the game?

Have you left your youthful dreams behind in service of deeper, more authentic ones? Or have you made a bad bargain by trading fulfillment for money or safety?

Are you putting out to the world what you desire? Are you receiving what you give? Are you giving what you receive?

It's true that some of our specific dreams and fantasies have expiration dates. For example, at a certain point in life, you may get too old to pursue your dream of being a professional football player or ballet dancer. But what is the intention behind the goal? Perhaps the intention is to challenge yourself physically with others who are doing the same. That's still attainable. What's calling you?

At a certain point, you can't change your childhood or years spent estranged from your parents. But you can bridge that gap now, healing any pain in your heart. What's bothering you?

You can't wipe away the debt you incurred from making bad financial decisions, but you can pay those forward into a redefined sense of abundance. What's inspiring you? What's calling you forth?

You are creating your legacy, every moment, every day, right now, and it's not only for others—it's the massive reservoir of momentum that you yourself get to draw upon as you walk your path.

What can you do today to align your legacy with your light?

Trusting What You Know

What if you still aren't sure what you should to do next in life? Maybe you know something is missing, but you can't quite figure out what. You sense there's more for you out there, but you don't know exactly what that is.

When this question comes up, we always share our experience with Mike. Mike is an accomplished manager and executive at a large multinational company. He came to us for a year of coaching a while back.

In our first meeting, he said something we hear a lot: "I'm proud of what I've done and who I am. I'm good at my job, and I'm proud of the opportunities it created for my family. But lately, it just isn't as interesting as it used to be. I'm on the road a lot, and I find myself wishing I could be home more as my kids get older."

Both of us wiped away tears as he talked. Looking at our own frequent flier cards, we could really relate to a lot of what he was saying. And to give Mike credit, he was already way more aware than many people we meet. He didn't need to diagnose that there might be something missing—he could feel it. He didn't need a Mack Truck wake-up call. He heard whispers that there was something more, and he decided to trust them. But he wanted help trying to figure out what the whispers were saying.

We cleared our calendars so we could spend a full day together in HeartSpace.

We started with a simple question: "What do you like to do?"

"Sure, okay," Mike said. "Well, not to be immodest, but I'm really excellent at management, setting goals and creating ownership in my team, creating buy-in around new products, and helping the team navigate transitions."

We listened politely and then said, "Maybe you didn't understand the question. You told us what you are *good* at regarding your job. What do you *like* to do? Without regard to work?"

Mike stared at us blankly. He was quiet for a moment. "Oh, I see." He paused. "It sounds silly, but I love traveling with my family. I love being a dad, and I love trying to get better at it. I love coaching football. If I could do anything, I'd do that more."

We looked at each other and back at Mike. We were surprised to see him frustrated. "Look, I'm sorry, but this doesn't help me! This just makes me *more* lost. I love coaching and I also love providing for my family. The two are really at odds, at least where I live—I'd have to take a 90 percent pay cut and leave behind three decades of work experience to be a coach, and that is directly at odds with providing for my family."

We were surprised at his frustration. "Mike," we said, "we're not jumping to the end here. We're not telling you to become a full-time high school football coach. We're just asking a question: What do you like?"

He relaxed and smiled. "Yeah, I get it. I guess I'm used to managing to results. Okay, what now?"

Listening to Your Wisdom

We asked Mike to take out a clean sheet of paper.

"What does your ideal role look like?" we asked.

"Ugh!" He groaned. "I told you! I have no idea. None of the roles I see and none of the positions I've interviewed for seem like a fit for me. And changing what I do at this point is so impractical anyway. It will never work."

We had lost him to discouragement again. We asked him to back up. "Don't tell us what you've found out there. On the blank sheet of paper, write out exactly what *you* want, whether you know it is out there or not."

He grumbled, but he put his head down and started writing. Amazingly, in only a few minutes he had a very, very specific list.

"What I'd love is an executive role at a middle-market company that is in consumer products, preferably in active lifestyles. It would be post-revenue, with a significant growth trajectory in front of it. I'd like to manage a team of high performers, so I'm looking for a place that has already attracted some experienced talent. And I'd like to travel less than two weeks a quarter, and nothing during the fall so I can coach. I don't necessarily need a pay increase, but I'd love an equity position."

He put down his paper, and we could tell he didn't understand why we were smiling at him.

"Mike," we said. "Did you hear that? You know *exactly* what you want!"

He looked at us and he looked at his piece of paper. "Oh shit," he laughed.

Within a few months Mike had identified a few firms that fit his criteria, interviewed at several, and secured a new position and promotion. He's now doing the most exciting work of his career—and is available to coach all season.

Believing in You

We've had this experience over and over—a client tells us that they have no idea what they want. When we get them to slow down, listen to themselves, and reflect, we find out they know *exactly* what they want. What seemed like "not knowing" was actually "not imagining it could be possible." But creating the space to become aware of what they want, reflect on the options, and explicitly enumerate them helps create the belief needed to manifest it.

When we helped Mike create a safe space for and *from* himself—from his fears, insecurities, worries, and negative self-talk—he was able to articulate his ideal life very succinctly. And you know what? It didn't sound fanciful or foolish. It didn't sound frivolous or irresponsible. And it certainly didn't sound unattainable.

It simply required Mike to listen to what he already knew, patiently, like he was his own best friend rather than his own worst critic. How would that change the way you talk to yourself?

As we've done this deep work of conscious leadership and living purpose, we've lived the experience we had with Mike again and again. Often, a person's dream isn't any more "unrealistic" than the life the person is living already. It's just different. And sometimes, it has been stored in the attic for so long that it simply must be dusted off a bit.

Experiences like the one with Mike have made us feel very differently than we used to feel about following one's true path. We used to think it took great courage and power to follow your own path. Now, we see that it is so much harder to try to continue to convince yourself to like a life that isn't everything you want it to be.

We're often told that following our dreams is silly, difficult, impractical, and full of hardship. And yet, after working with thousands of people who have successfully climbed the ladder—only to get to the top and wonder "Is this all there is?"—we actually think that being someone you *aren't* is the hardest task of all.

We all go in and out of alignment throughout our lives. What fulfillment means changes for each of us as we grow. During the times we end up out of alignment with ourselves, it takes its toll—physically, mentally, and spiritually. It's one reason, we believe, that so many people have grown accustomed to taking antidepressants, alcohol, blood thinners, statins, reflux medications—you name it.

There's a significant "counter-passion" movement in business literature right now. We've been watching a growing number of articles and videos urging people to "do what they like, not what they love." The core idea of this movement is that "following your passion" sets people up for failure and disappointment, and that unrealistically high expectations sit at the center of a great deal of modern malaise. The argument goes that a healthier life comes from doing what will provide for you and your family, and saving passion for the weekends.

We can't help but think that kind of advice is quite self-serving for the consultants and business executives who are offering it up. After a few years of massive change, quarantines, lockdowns, and upheaval, more people than ever are realizing, "I want more from life." Money isn't enough to keep people working at jobs they don't really like. Money certainly isn't enough to keep people working at jobs they weren't fairly compensated for in the first place.

Following your dreams seems silly to most people because they simply don't know how to do it. It seems difficult to most people because they've never practiced it. It feels impractical because they can't imagine trading a "sure" paycheck doing something that is somewhat interesting for an uncertain paycheck doing something that is deeply captivating. (Never mind that many people who have a "sure" paycheck suddenly find themselves on the receiving end of mass layoffs, firings, and corporate downsizing.)

Think about it this way: Are you more secure relying on yourself, or more secure relying on the whims and decisions of a business or boss, over which you have no control? There are plenty of things you can't control in your life. How you spend your time is one of the few choices you really have.

The river goes where the river flows—does it really make sense to hand your only paddle to someone else?

Making Space for Yourself

Have you ever been sitting next to a loud noise—a generator, a fan, a truck, a construction site—as you were trying to read or meet or work?

At first, it is annoying and disruptive. "I can't hear myself think!" you say.

But you must do your work, so you do your best to ignore the racket. You start to make progress with your meeting or report or project, and as you do, you get into a zone. The background noise becomes something you get used to.

Then, suddenly, the noise finally stops. The fan turns off or the construction workers head to lunch. Maybe you don't even consciously notice the new silence with your ears at first—you sense it in your body before you can identify what happened. You detect a sense of open space. Then you realize how *loud* it had been just moments ago. Everything is not only quieter but calmer. You have more room to think. You have more headroom to *be*. You notice things you couldn't hear before: Birds outside. A fountain in the garden. Kids playing down the block.

When you hear yourself say, "I'm ready for more," that's kind of like the noise turning off. Suddenly, you have more room. New things become apparent to you.

Often, we've seen that these calm, quiet revelations are alarming. Our clients' first reaction is often to fill the space with more noise: trying to figure out what's next, striving to change their path, worrying they've missed the boat, regretting how they've spent their time, or fearing that life has passed them by.

You don't need any of that. You just need to make some space for yourself. You don't need much—just enough for four lights to remind you:

    I.   You are light.

    II.   Your light is always on.

    III.   You only have to see what is right in front of you.

    IV.   There's a larger light guiding you.

Make some room to let your own light in. You'll be amazed at who you become.

You live one life. We can't wait to see what you do with yours.

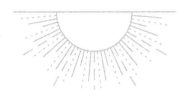

About the Authors

Jennifer Mulholland is a third-generation female entrepreneur, business strategist, executive coach, and spiritual teacher passionate about helping individuals and organizations reach their full potential. Since she was a young girl, she's been dedicated and driven to help raise the consciousness of people on the planet, which has fueled her training in human performance, business consulting, technology, psychology, exercise and sports science, mental health, and healing.

As the co-owner of Plenty Consulting, Jennifer fuses business savvy with spiritual alchemy to catalyze holistic growth for leaders and organizations alike in business strategy, conscious leadership, team performance, innovation, and cultural wellbeing.

She is a certified Reiki and Theta healer trained in shamanic and energy medicine and intuitive development. Jennifer has a B.S. degree from the University of Utah in Exercise and Sports Science, Psychology, and Coaching. In addition to her mental pursuits, Jennifer is a multi-sport athlete and a former two-sport Division I athlete at the University of Delaware, playing lacrosse and field hockey. Two decades ago, she founded a nonprofit organization and brought women's lacrosse to Utah.

Before Plenty, Jennifer founded three technology, wellbeing, and executive coaching companies focused on bridging the gap between information and impact. For nearly ten years, she worked in the corporate sector as General Manager of Consulting Services and Chief Innovation Officer at SunGard (now called Ellucian), a Fortune 500 technology company.

A nature lover and Park City, Utah, resident for three decades, Jennifer cherishes spending time outdoors with her husband, two children, and goldendoodle. She enjoys skiing deep powder, doing hot yoga, hiking the mountain trails, writing, channeling meditations, leading sacred ceremonies, and cheffing up healthy meals for her friends and loved ones.

Jeff Shuck lives with his wife Jeanie in Michigan City, Indiana—about halfway between Chicago and South Bend. They are the proud parents of four amazing children.

A lifelong entrepreneur, idealist, wonderer, and wanderer, Jeff has founded three businesses. His early career focused on leadership development for college students. He spent three tough but gratifying years as a professional singer, songwriter, and owner of a small independent record label, One Room Schoolhouse Music.

After his mom died of cancer when he was 29, Jeff further focused his career on the ideals of service, compassion, and positive change. In 2002, he and two partners co-founded the nation's premier event fundraising firm, Event 360, and he served for twelve years as the company's CEO. Event 360 raised hundreds of millions of dollars for charity during his tenure.

Jeff founded Plenty in 2013 to broaden beyond fundraising and work more directly with leaders, teams, and organizations to create a better world. Over the last ten years, Plenty has worked with hundreds of for-profit and nonprofit businesses and thousands of conscious leaders. His work on social impact, leadership, and positive change has been featured in the *Wall Street Journal*, *Marketplace*, *Fatherly*, and the *Stanford Social Innovation Review*.

Jeff is an avid musician, composer, writer, reader, and weight-lifter. He loves water, red wine, and role-playing games in equal measure. Jeff graduated Phi Beta Kappa from the University of Rochester and holds master's degrees in business administration and predictive analytics from Northwestern University.

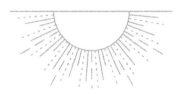

Thank You

Learning to lead with light in work and life can be easy, fulfilling, and enriching. At times, it can also be challenging, frustrating, and contracting! So here are some additional resources we've created to help illuminate the way.

To become more aware of your light, aligned in your leadership, and intentional in your growth, check out our **Lantern Leadership Assessment**, which builds on the principles in this book, www.plentyconsulting.com/the-lantern-leadership-assessment.

If you're ready to go deeper into the Four Lights of Conscious Leadership with other conscious leaders, we'd love to have you join us at Lantern, our Retreat for Conscious Leaders! Held at HeartSpace, our private retreat center in beautiful Park City, Utah, we'll dive into the curriculum explored in this book to equip you with mindful leadership strategies, elevated consciousness, and increased confidence. Learn more and register at www.plentyconsulting.com/lantern-leadership-retreat.

Visit our **website** for new blog posts, readings, meditations, and more (www.plentyconsulting.com). Our website also has links to where to find us on most of the major social networks.

Subscribe to our **free e-newsletter** featuring inspiring anecdotes, updates on our work with conscious leaders, our latest

meditations, podcast episodes, and more (www.plentyconsulting
.com/subscribe).

Tune in to our **podcast**, *Plenty for Everyone*, where we talk with
conscious leaders like you to explore abundance in work and life,
fulfillment in head and heart, and ways we can all work together
to make this world a better place. Subscribe on Apple Podcasts,
Spotify, Google, and all the other major podcast services, and
find all the latest episodes at www.plentyconsulting.com/podcast.

Listen to our **guided meditations,** a core conscious leadership
practice and a deep joy to share, featuring Jennifer's gifted channeled words and Jeff's beautiful music. Tune in to open your
heart, expand your thinking, and align with your light. You can
find our meditations on Insight Timer and on our website at
www.plentyconsulting.com/meditations.

You can find **videos** of our podcast episodes, meditations,
insight, and more at www.youtube.com/@PlentyConsulting.

And if you're looking for something deeper for yourself,
your team, or your organization, we offer conscious leadership
coaching, services, and keynotes for businesses and nonprofits of all sizes. You can contact us to find out more at www
.plentyconsulting.com/contact-us.

We're here to help you grow!

Printed in the USA
CPSIA information can be obtained
at www.ICGtesting.com
LVHW041609230324
774945LV00013B/57/J

9 781951 692384